The Little Scribe

A catalogue record of this book is available from the British Library

First Edition: November 2005

ISBN: 1-84375-180-1

To order additional copies of this book please visit:
http://www.upso.co.uk/ronbateman

Published by: UPSO Ltd
5 Stirling Road, Castleham Business Park,
St Leonards-on-Sea, East Sussex TN38 9NW United Kingdom
Tel: 01424 853349 Fax: 0870 191 3991
Email: info@upso.co.uk   Web: http://www.upso.co.uk

Thoughts are precious gems, may you find them in this little book.

Sincerely Yours.

R. Bateman

" The Little Scribe"

The Little Scribe

by

Ron Bateman

UPSO

A few words of explanation regarding the writings in this little volume.

In March 2000, my life-long friend and companion died, and soon afterwards I was 'prompted' to sit down and write.

What I wrote surprised me. I was 'told' via these writings that they would come from Brothers, who belong to what is known as 'The White Brotherhood'; that they would work through Brian, my companion; and that I was to be the last link in the chain as it were, for their Teachings.

I am often awakened in the early hours and I go to my study and write quickly for about an hour or so, then I go back to bed and sleep.

When I get up in the morning, I read what has been written and then record it on a cassette then I listen to, and hopefully learn from, what has been written.

I am just the scribe and can take no credit for what is written, but I feel very privileged to be part of this ongoing teaching and am very grateful to my Brothers and to Brian.

To those of you who have read this little volume, I hope the words of comfort have helped you. To those who are searching, I trust you have found what you were looking for.

May the Blessings of the One on High be with you now and always.

I dedicate this book to Brian, who is the inspiration for it, and to Irene, without whose help and encouragement this book could not have been written.

Thank you.

Ron Bateman
"The Little Scribe"

Chapter 1

May 6th 2003

What Lies Ahead?

As we go through life there are times when we stop to think and then take stock of where we are, where we have been, and where we are going.

These are milestones as it were, in ones life and each one represents not only a passage of time but also a period of learning. Even if that had not occurred to us as such!

As a child, much of our so-called learning takes place in school; 'life' as such has not really touched us. There are always meals upon the table, someone to take care of troubles when they arise, in fact more or less a normal childhood.

It is when we have to earn a living in the real world that life's lessons really begin.

There are DECISIONS to be made, whether right or wrong, and the consequences have to be borne.

No one to wipe away a tear! You are on your own two feet, for what it is worth!

Looking back you can see perhaps where you went wrong and know that should that occasion arise again, you would handle it differently.

You see you are learning without realising the significance of it. This then is *your* life and it's now up to you what you make of it.

And so it goes on. You get older, perhaps a little wiser, and then you are pulled up with a start! Where have all those years gone?

What lies ahead? Old age? With all its problems! What have you done with your life? Are you prepared for the next phase when it arrives? The next phase is one of inevitability, and its name is *Death*!

What are your thoughts about it? (If any!!!)

Has what you have learned fitted you for this next step upon the upward path? Did you really think that this life of yours had any relevance to the coming one?

Well, yes it has, for you have become, perhaps without knowing it, a *character* and this character part of you is what you will 'carry over' to the next part of your ONGOING life. For it is ongoing my friend. It does NOT stop just because you have left behind a worn out garment called 'your body'! You now will be given, as it were, another one. One that you have been using without realising it all these years that you spent upon Earth.

It is called your 'spirit'. It is the *real you* and not that worn out shell that you used to think of as you. You are far more complex than just one, for in truth it is one of *many* that you will inhabit in your journey back to the source of your creation.

We are all the same, you are NO DIFFERENT, we all have to pass along this pathway towards what we term our goal in 'life'; for this *life* is continuous, believe me.

So now you begin to wonder what this new life cycle is all about and you want to embark upon it.

Sadly there is NO alternative. You have NO SAY in the matter. Your life has been planned, and you think: "by whom, don't I have any say?"

You have had, my friend. For it was YOU who did the planning before you embarked upon the journey that started out on Earth.

Perhaps you don't believe that? Well it is the TRUTH whether you see it as such, or not. You didn't just *happen* when you were born. You had seen previously upon the plane of Spirit understanding, what this life of yours was for.

It was for the progression, you knew what it was that was needed for you to become a more *rounded being*; a being of *light*, as we all are in the beginning.

But then we are not aware of who and what we are. We are, as it were, in the *embryonic stage*; waiting. Waiting for the moment when life is bestowed *within* us so that a soul is born, a soul is created, we are now part of the supreme *Creator*, not yet aware of that for we are in a sense 'sleeping'. It is when we are 'awakened' that we begin to know that we are more than what we seem to be.

That is the start of our downward journey through all the spheres, to one day return from the lowest one - called Earth - back through those spheres that were once our homes for a while; and as we return, we can see where we have been and why. As we tarry once more upon familiar territory we know *who we are*; and we know that we are nearing our journey's end.

Not yet though, for there is still some way to go before we can, shall we say, qualify for the title of one of God's *co-workers*; for that has been our desire from the beginning.

The journey has been long and has taken many, many lives on many, many spheres of existence to bring us eventually back to the Creative principal we call "GOD".

So you see, that sojourn upon Earth was worthwhile. It is indeed needed for our education to make us *think*. And when I say *think*, I really mean *thought*. That is, thought made positive.

It seems a pity that when we are young we are not taught more about what this life is for and why we are living it. In the West, religious teaching does not encourage people to question and seek the inner meaning of what life is really for.

We are here to *learn*, and learning means our everyday life; of how we treat those with whom we come into contact. Learn to love yourself and then you learn how to love others. For it is LOVE in it's universal sense that keeps this world turning. We all *matter*; which means we all *matter* to God.

Believe that and know that we are all a part of Him as He is part of us. So treat each other as if you were giving to God the love that He has given you. In doing that you are loving your neighbour as yourself.

You have reached a milestone. Reflect, learn and then go forward in the knowledge that what you do is important. You are here to learn. In the learning you are growing nearer to God. Let Him into your life for it was He who gave it to you in the first place.

Return it to Him by loving one another. See in them the God within and know that that is what living a good life is all about.

Chapter 2

May 7th 2003

The Spirit World

What is it that seems to intrigue most people about the World of the Spirit?

It is what happens on a day-to-day basis. They wonder, do we work? Do we sit around and look pious? Do we *do* anything?

Well, of course we *do*. Life goes on here as it did, or rather *does*, when one is on the Earth plane. Of course there are differences. We don't *work* for a living.

When we say 'work' we do mean what is said. There are forms of what is termed 'manual work'. You wonder at that, for you are thinking how can Spirit forms do *manual work*?!

Your manual style of work is not in the same *league* as ours. Our manual work does consist of using our hands and arms; but they are used by thought, and not sheer physical labour. Though the outcome is the same.

Surprises you no doubt, for you imagine that physical manual work can only be confined to the people of the Earth.

Lesson number one: our world to us is just as *physical*, if that is the correct word, as yours is to you. We do not live on a sphere of whispy, 'airy-fairy' elements. Our 'things' are solid to the touch as we are to each other. We move as you do, but with far greater ease of movement. Yes we can *glide,* if you wish to call it that, when we desire. But on the whole, gentle movement we find is quite sufficient for our 'everyday' activity.

Now, that will make you sit up and think "everyday activity". What does he mean by that, I wonder?

Everyday activity is when we are at our 'workplace'. Not a factory as such, not even a place of business; though there are 'places' where *business* is taught; that is, the principles of business and not the actual making of 'money'. Money is not required here, though there is a form of *exchange* in certain areas. There are what you know of as *markets*; these are purely for those people who need to re-adjust to our way of living, but who are, shall we say, still sort of Earth-bound in their thinking.

Just because you have TRANSFERRED to this new life it doesn't fall into place immediately, it takes what you call time. Time to adjust and understand that what was and seemed important upon the Earth need not be relevant here! Here you are shown how to manipulate thought patterns so that what is required, though not always *needed*, can be formed into a semblance of reality: which, incidentally, is *real* in every sense of the word.

Though reality here, as you will find out, is not quite the same as upon the Earth plane! There, reality is what you perceive all around you. What you touch, what you eat, what you 'put on'. Here reality is a form that can be termed 'illusion', for it need not be 'permanent'; and yet it does not 'disintegrate', it just returns to its 'source' – which is 'mind substance'.

Rather a lot for you to take in we feel at present. But it is true, as you will one day find out for yourselves.

Thought has to be 'regulated', and that means learning how to use it 'constructively'.

All this has to be *taught* and *learnt*; all part of this, your new *growth life*.

Yes, in answer to your thought, we do have gardens and yes we do grow what is called 'produce', though not of the material substance as upon Earth. Our produce is for the purpose of 'knowledge'. There are areas put aside where 'produce' is grown for its medicinal purposes!

We study to evaluate what can be achieved by the growing of various forms of 'culture'. These substances are used in parts of our globe and 'others', including your Earth plane; though you are not yet aware of it! Where do you think a 'new found species' has come from when it is discovered upon Earth? It has its origins on our plane first and then transported to yours when we feel it would be of use to you.

All of this 'work' needs people who are dedicated to the creation of various forms of 'growth culture'. We study the organisms of creation and manipulate them in our experiments. This is just one of the many studies that you would term as 'work'.

You wonder what else we do as well as garden culture growth. For not all people here are of that 'inclination'.

There are 'schools' for the promotion of 'ideas'. Ideas that can be put to practical use both here and 'elsewhere', if you get our meaning.

Our world is not confined to just 'ourselves', we 'go' where we are required to and so what we 'create' can be used whenever it is needed. It can take the form of a 'blueprint' that can be implanted upon the thought pattern of, shall we say, a scientist or an inventor upon your planet and *others*.

Our creative sources are not confined to just our own world. We are part of the Universe of Life as you are, and so we play our part in its evolutionary process.

Creation is forever ongoing: it is never still. Even your world is undergoing more 'creation'. It is being altered to suit the evolutionary process, as are many more that, at present, are not known about by those upon the Earth.

But they will, in time!

Your world is an important training ground for *the present*. Now that should give you a clue as to what we mean!

There are others that are, shall we say, 'waiting in the wings' until they are ready to take your place eventually.

No you will not disappear, you will be amalgamated with another one 'higher' than your own where your ideas will be used and evaluated into a higher form of life. You will no longer be considered a dense planet of heavy atmosphere, but one of light and of a spiritual nature. Still a learning ground, but for those of a higher order.

But that, dear friends, is not even in the distant future, it is beyond that!

We return to our beginning of this night's discourse. Life upon our sphere is one of activity, and yes, still one of learning. But we learn to pass on our knowledge to those ready to receive it and put it to the proper use for which it is intended. We all depend upon each other, for that is what evolution is all about. We are a planet of creative principles, as you are. But where we differ is that we create for constructive ideas, and not destructive as you seem to do. Your inventions always seem to possess a good and bad side, and it seems to us that the bad predominates!

Learn to create in harmony with Nature, and that means work within the NATURAL laws of the Universe. With them and not against them

These laws apply to everything and were put in place as guidelines for right living. Learn to live by them and you will find that life will once more take upon itself what you termed 'The Golden Age'. We will now bid you "Farewell", we will come back to this subject again for there is still much for us to tell you about our way of Life which one day will be yours also.

Chapter 3

May 8th 2003

Our Lives

W hat is it that we can say to you about 'lives'? We use that word advisedly for one life would never be sufficient for our journey back to the creative source! We have so much not only to learn but also to 'unlock', for memories are permanent reminders of things past that are still relevant to today's thinking.

That, dear Brother, goes for all of us. That is, those who think 'deeply', for not all thought goes beyond 'shallow thought'. That is not to say shallow means what you upon Earth think it does! It just means thoughts that do not go beneath the surface but rather remain hovering above it! People on the whole do not wish to think too deeply about what the real or inner life means to them. For when, or rather *if*, they do it makes them feel dissatisfied; and most people would rather not feel that dissatisfaction for if they did then they would have to change not only their behaviour but also their entire thought patterns. For thoughts do become patterns, without people actually realising it. They become a way of life. In other words, they are 'habit forming', and when a habit is, shall we say, 'pleasant and not demanding' then who wants to change it for something that requires definite effort and perhaps will alter their present lifestyle. But if they only realised it, that effort would result in rewards of untold worth, not necessarily for the physical body, but for the Spirit that dwells within. Though to be more precise, the Spirit as you call it does *not* remain permanently within your body shell. 'It', or rather this 'other you' does also have a life of its own as well as having the duty, as it were, to keep a check on you; its temporary companion, its physical body!

You now begin to see that you are not one, not even two, but in fact many more than that, all making up the same one, the one known as 'Soul'.

Soul is often talked about, and quite loosely in fact. You hear people say "Oh, poor old soul", or "What a lovely soul", or then again "How does a person manage to keep body and soul together these days".

You see the word 'Soul' is not properly understood. 'It' is *not* a replica of the human body: it is beyond that. For it is the 'source' of the creations that go to make us who and what we are. Soul is the manifested essence of the Divine Creative Principle, that part of the one you call God that has allowed Himself to be manifested as a being of light, with all of the God-like principles within it. Not knowing, but willing to learn. For we must eventually return to that Divine essence and, yes, 'give account of ourselves'. Remember the parable of Jesus regarding the 'talents'. Do not bury them in the hope that when they are unearthed they will have multiplied. *They will not.* In fact they may even have disappeared completely back to the dust from which they came.

You are endowed with far more than you can ever know. But do not confuse 'talent' with what to some people means 'artistic ability'. For talent can encompass many, many aspects. In fact, to name just one, being and living a good life is a talent in itself. For if you truly and sincerely lead a life of goodness, which means loving your neighbour as yourself, you are in fact bringing forth many talents, not only within yourself but in others also.

Who knows what just a word or gesture can mean to someone who may be in despair, lonely, or who has 'lost their way in life'. *Your* talent for living has multiplied in others what had perhaps been hidden for a very long time.

So you see dear friends, the word 'talent' has so many meanings, hasn't it? Look within yourselves, you may be agreeably surprised at what you discover. *Your Spirit* is the main outlet for this elusive talent. Accept what 'it' has to give to you, for the Spirit is your main link with the other 'you', those 'you' who will one day become what the Soul essence has given and has now required its return: not just one hundred fold, but many times that number! You are to become a co-worker with the *Ones on High*. Think upon that. *Ones On High*. They have attained this status by effort, it wasn't just *given* out to them. They earned it, just as you can and, we say, *will*. We are all the same, we all start out as aspects of the One Creator. Let us show Him that His vision of a brotherhood of all his creations is possible. For we are part of Him, are we not? And that part is God Himself given in and with *love*. So that is how we should live our various lives, with *love* for Him and for our Brothers. For we are all Brothers, aren't we?

We call upon God as 'Our Father' and so we are brothers in truth. That is how we should treat and be treated. It is the Spirit that we should see in each other, and the Spirit knows *NO* colour boundaries, for the Spirit is *all colours* and yet is *NONE*.

Release that Spirit consciousness within you, try to live as *one body*, for you are, if you did but know it. It just requires thought and effort, and we have been given those talents, have we not? Use them to see how they will multiply and bring forth fruit in abundance. Each life that you will live, either upon the Earth plane or in one of the many spheres that await you, will bring you nearer to the goal that we all seek. Union with the Creator of All that there is and ever has been and always will.

Live and learn and love, for that is what our lives are all about.

They were born in love, the love of our Father, let us learn to love Him back. That is truly loving one another as we know we should. It is possible, it can be done. Ask and it shall be given to you to give to others. Let this and other lives be a fitting tribute to the Almighty.

Chapter 4

May 9th 2003

Youth

So much speculation goes on in the minds of the young people upon your planet at this time. They are, shall we say, 'fed up' with all of the old fashioned platitudes, they want proof, if any, of what comes after, when this life upon the Earth plane comes to an end. They *know* that there *must* be more to life than just the one that they are now living. So they turn to some of those people who they think can give them answers to the many questions that bother them.

Unfortunately, many of these so-called religious cults that have sprung up only pose more questions than the feeble answers they give.

If they only knew what harm they do to those young and impressionable minds. Sometimes the harm done is irreparable on your world of existence. It is then left to *us* to try to put together the broken minds and bodies of those youngsters when, so often, they are catapulted into the next sphere with absolutely no idea of where they are, and what is not only happening to them, but what has actually happened to them to put them where they find themselves.

They 'come over' angry, frustrated and bitter, seeking to blame someone or something, but never themselves! It takes us a long time to penetrate this apathy that surrounds them and we cannot help them by explaining to them that it is the consequence of their own behaviour patterns, all that concerns them is returning to Earth as soon as possible. We take them, sometimes quite forcibly, to an area upon our side of our planet which is put aside for what you would call 'detoxification', they are put into a trance-like sleep, but their subconscious is awakened. This is how we deal with them to start with. We feed the subconscious with information of a positive nature. We do *not* condemn or condone what they have been guilty of doing to themselves and others, for their actions cause reactions to those who have been around them. We gradually see that they are responding to our ministrations and when we deem it is right, we 'bring them back' from their sleep-state. They are still bewildered, but they are more passive and receptive to what we are teaching them.

Little by little they begin to see that what they thought was permissible is not. When they are mentally stronger they are taken to a place where they are shown their behaviour when upon the Earth plane. This is in the form of a cinematograph film. They are alone when viewing this film, for it is very traumatic. They see how their lifestyle has affected others as well as themselves. Then they are shown what has become of those friends and so-called close friends, and the change in the person is quite dramatic. If they truly repent of their past actions they are given a choice. If these people with whom they were in contact when on Earth are still alive and in need of help, then the one who has now shown remorse is allowed, under our supervision – and that means with a guide and helper – to revisit the Earth plane in Spirit form and endeavour to help upon the mental plane those who they seek to help, and put right what they did when still alive.

This takes a lot of what you would call 'guts'. It is not an easy task and is not always successful. But when it is, then there is satisfaction all round. Such a lot of time has been wasted with these young souls; lives blighted by drugs and the so-called life of *fun* that these youngsters seem to think is all there is to life.

Example is what is needed for these young people when upon Earth. 'Role models' are what you like to call them. *Jesus* is one, if they could only see it. But so many young people are not shown that he was flesh and blood the same as all of us, who, in spite of everything, lived a good and proper life. It was not easy then, it never has been, but that is not to say that living a good and decent life cannot be achieved by those alive today. It is learning about the good things in life, the things that will fit you for the life to come. You don't want to be continually coming back to Earth to learn lessons that you have neglected to learn in the first place. Look beyond this physical existence to the glorious lives that await us all. Things cannot be put off indefinitely, we all have to know who we really are and why we are here. It's all a matter of priority. Look to the future and know that the *now* is what the future will hold for you.

Teach your young souls the true values in life. Start when they are impressionable. Show them that being good is its own reward and that the opposite only ends in doom. It is not only the youngsters who are at fault. The adults are equally to blame for it is their responsibility to show by example that living a decent life – and that means an *unselfish* one – is what living is all about. Love yourself and then one another with true brotherly love, we are all dependent upon each other, accept that fact and go forward. Bring *God* back to the classrooms and He will stay with the child throughout his adult life. We need *God* more than He needs us; and yet we are all precious to Him for after all we are all His children, and he is our Father, isn't he?

The children of today are the future generations of this Earth. See to it that they become citizens of the world and not just one country in particular, for your world is shrinking rapidly and man cannot remain an *island* indefinitely.

Chapter 5

May 10th 2003

Memories

We have spoken to you before regarding our life upon the Spirit realm, but we have hardly touched on the subject of those souls who are, shall we say, in 'transit'. By which we mean, those who are here on a temporary basis. They are here for rest and recuperation before they are to once more incarnate upon the Earth plane for another round of lessons to be learnt and debts to be paid.

Now that will cause you to think. But looking at it dispassionately, you can see the logic of that statement. As we travel along Earth's pathway we naturally encounter many, many souls who are doing the same. That is, they are 'living' and so in that life they will make mistakes. They may create enemies. Not, shall we say, of the war-like variety, but those who are incompatible in one way or another. All of these encounters are registered upon what *one* may call a person's life pattern. They have left their mark as have you. Some of these acquaintances do not register in a particular way and so can, as it were, be dismissed; for they do not create a permanent mark upon another's life. Then there are those who are important: relatives, loved ones, those from previous lives who have made an impression. These are the ones who we have 'come back' to either make amends to or are part of what is known on the Earth as 'one's karma'. You are bound to these others until the ties can either be *broken* or *mended*. This is the reason for those souls that we have mentioned who, upon release from the physical body, are 'visitors' to the world of Spirit and are not permanent residents, so to speak.

Once they have had their 'rest and recuperation', they are put aside for the main purpose of re-educating those who will one day reincarnate upon the Earth. But before that can take place they have to be shown why this is necessary for them. If they do not understand why they have to return, then that incarnation would not be of value to them, would it?

They are, as it were, allowed to view in depth their past life with all its vices and virtues. They are then able to assess for themselves what they need to do about it. And now we come to a part that is quite a challenge for them. Once they have decided what is needed, they are given the choice of who and what they *wish* to become and where upon Earth's globe they think this new incarnation would be of most benefit to them. They are shown a number of 'options'. They may, for instance, favour more than one 'option' and so they are allowed to 'live' these options.

Here we will explain the procedure.

They themselves are put into a deep sleep-like state; in the meantime their preferred options are put into what you would call a moving picture. A complete life, from the cradle to the grave.

Once these picture plays have been assembled, the one to whom they refer is awakened. They are then shown these films one by one. They are made aware that the main character in these films is themselves, so they can observe in detail the life that could await them.

Once they have decided upon the one that they feel is the right one for them, they are returned to their sleep-state. The one that is decided on is put aside: that is the film version, the others are just destroyed.

This first version is kept for reference in the archives that are put aside for that purpose. That soul whose life this is to be is once more awakened, but has no knowledge of what has transpired. They are, as it were, allowed their freedom to resume, shall we say, their 'holiday' until the time arrives when their return to Earth is due. All preparations have been made for their new life to continue. They are now shown once more the film version of their life to come. Now is the time for them to assess this coming life. If they feel certain changes should be made they are *noted*, but the film is not altered.

This is what the individual will have to adjust when their new life upon Earth is being lived!

Now *all memories* of what they have seen are removed before they depart for their new existence. In some cases these memories are not completely eradicated and so during their new lifetime they have feelings of somehow having done certain things before; but cannot remember when or where and often put them down to the dream-state. But those who are now the 'thinkers' can tap into those past memories and so perhaps can overcome a difficult situation that may have arisen, they have in fact been able to 'make the change' that they talked about before they came back to their new life.

This then is now put into the film record that has been stored away until the time comes when they are back upon the realm of Spirit and are reviewing their life once again!

They have been able to adjust their karma while upon Earth and so that is now taken into consideration and will benefit them in no uncertain terms. They *are* learning, and that is what all these lives are all about. Another step forward and not backward, as is often the case.

Once we have taken that forward step, and know why we have, we have learnt a valuable lesson. That is: how we progress. Our lives, whether upon Earth or in the world of Spirit or even perhaps 'elsewhere' if applicable, are all for a purpose. Once we accept that then we can progress more rapidly. Learn to live life and in the living we are learning all the time. We all have to travel these paths, some quicker than others, but eventually we shall all get to where we know we belong. And if we can help someone on the way with knowledge of what we have learnt, then we truly are living the life we were intended to.

We feel that we will leave you on that note!

Chapter 6

May 11th 2003

The Truth

Yes dear Brother, we are here and we will speak with you. As a searcher after the truth you must always make sure that what you impart to others is the Truth, as far as you are aware of it. For truth can be twisted by those who wish to confuse others. Not all so-called 'teachers' are either in possession of the truth; or in some cases, they do *not* wish the 'true truth' to be known. They wish to keep it to themselves for it gives them a sense of power, which if they did but realise it is a 'false power'. For in time they will be seen for what they really are: 'wolves in sheep's clothing'.

There are many in the world today, and here we must be honest and say that not all of them, who impart doctrines that are to say not only false, but wayward in the extreme. They do not realise what harm they are doing. Or perhaps they do, which makes it doubly doubtful for anyone who is gullible enough to take in all that they are being 'fed'. For it is a form of 'food' that they are being given and it is POISONOUS in the extreme. Whenever anyone tells you that it is the truth that they are telling you, think about it hard before you accept it. That, dear friend, goes for *us* as well! If you in yourself cannot go along with what is being said then do not hesitate to question the validity of statements, or reserve your judgement until you can, in the quietude of your own home, ponder upon what has been told to you and ask for inner guidance. That really means 'asking yourself' for ultimately you must be the judge of what you have either *heard* or *read*.

No one is infallible, we all put our own interpretation on what we are saying or thinking and who is to say that our interpretation is the correct one. Circumstances, and that means 'timescale' can sometimes alter one's perception of what has always been thought of as a TRUTH! That is not to say that it wasn't the *truth then*. But times change. Our whole outlook can alter even in a matter of a few years, or even weeks come to that. Always keep an 'open mind' on any given subject. If what has been said or read strikes a chord within you, then go along with it, but do *not* be dogmatic about it. Who knows, another word or book may open up a new wave of thought processes that give you a different outlook on what you had previously been informed.

You see dear friend, we are always learning, and we hope progressing, each *thought* that we *think* and that is when we are thinking *deeply* should be analysed before accepting it as, shall we say, *gospel!* So much in the past was thought of in those terms and the very idea of criticising or not even wholly believing what had been told one would have labelled them as outcast and disbeliever, just because they were using their God given ability to think for themselves.

People in the past somehow thought that if you questioned what was termed 'Holy', God would smite you in some way or a disaster would befall you. Thank goodness that in this day and age we think quite differently. But that still doesn't mean to say that we must ignore all that has been written or said in bygone days. Just learn to differentiate between what was just folklore and what had its basis in the *truth of the past*.

Truth can mean so many different things to so many different people, and here we are speaking of those of different religions or cultures. Always remember that no *one religion* has all of the truth. To those who practice it, it may seem that their group has it. But then those others feel that they too have the Truth, so who is to say which one is right? We certainly cannot answer that question and so we leave it to God. Who better to ask for an answer? He will answer you via your inward thoughts, if you learn to be, as we said, 'open-minded'. Nothing is quite what it seems, either in your life or in ours! Learn to *see* with your *inner eye;* and you do understand what we say we know.

So the lesson to be learnt is *be true to yourself.* Listen to others' points of view and then make up your own mind, especially if you are asked for your opinion which usually means that the other person expects you to agree with them. Very few people are brave enough to listen to another person's adverse criticism. But, if they have learned the valuable lesson of being 'open minded' about all things, they will not be upset and will perhaps find in your viewpoint a different perspective of what they had come to accept as 'sacrosanct'. But remember, never force your opinions upon others, better to keep a 'still tongue' in what is termed a 'wise head'!

We return to our beginning of this discourse. Do not feel that you have to experiment with various groups of this, so-called, 'new age culture', for half of them are just trying to recapture what should remain dead and buried and they do not realise what a can of worms they may release upon an 'unsuspecting' congregation!

We feel that we have given you plenty to think upon, just remember the truth lies within you, search your inner being of light and then let it shine forth for all to see. You can become a beacon of Truth just by being who you are. A child of God, for that is a **truth** that no one can deny.

Chapter 7

May 13th 2003

Thoughts

Thoughts are wonderful things, are they not? You have a *thought* and sometimes wonder where it came from. Was it within your own mind or did it come from outside your being? Well I think you know the answer to that one.

Thoughts as such are all around us, yes even upon our sphere, they are not confined to yours, for 'they' are electrical currents that exist all over the 'universe'. That probably makes you wonder, do 'thoughts' from outside of your known galaxy impinge upon those of your world? Well, the answer to that is *yes* and *no*! We are not being ambiguous in that reply. For thoughts are, shall we say, 'regulated'. Imagine 'waves' that form definite cycles. Almost like the tracks of one of your 'disks' that you place upon your machines. Remember the old-fashioned gramophone records? You placed the needle upon the first groove and then the music started, but if you were to raise the needle arm and place it further along the record, you would then get either a different part of the music being played, or even a completely different piece altogether! Same record but in a different groove a different sound. That is how your thought 'waves' behave. You may quite innocently 'tap' into a 'groove' that will give you a thought that could astonish you, one that would perhaps make you sit up and think. Where did that thought come from, I wonder?!

You see, dear friend, the whole of creation is made up of electrical currents and impulses, and yes even, shall we say, 'molecules' that can be 'manipulated' by a thought process to become positive 'realities' that do exist outside of the human or Spirit body. We said that thought waves from the atmosphere, that is shall we say, from another 'planet' can be intercepted if the right procedure is known and more importantly, understood. It is like the breaking of a 'code' that is there waiting to be understood.

As we have said, all life forms are made up of electrical impulses, that is why some people, and yes animals, can be affected in the change of the atmosphere when perhaps there is a sudden 'charge' or change in the electrical wave lengths. We are 'protected' in a way, so that not all electrical currents can affect us adversely, but some people seem to behave almost like a 'magnet' and so that when a change in the atmosphere occurs they 'attract it'. And so are somewhat affected by it, not always upsetting them, they just feel 'different'. Some react by feeling 'on edge' while others may get a feeling of excitement or expectation. Some may even feel extremely drowsy and want to sleep, it's as if they are being drained of their 'life force'. This doesn't last, but your scientific bodies do not as yet understand all the elements that go to make up what is known as a human being.

When, and even *if*, they ever do, then they would be in possession of a wonderful tool. For they could then learn how to regulate the mode of living by being able to harness this life giving force of energy and so pass it on to those who are either lacking it or those who maybe have more than they need. It can then be regulated for their benefit. There is so much for Man to learn, not only about the universe in which he lives but also about *himself*. Once he understands himself, and that means not only his physical vehicle but more importantly the 'one' that motivates it, then he will be well on the road to discovering the reason for his being upon this lower planet of learning and understanding.

Other planets or worlds in your universe have acquired some of this knowledge already that is why they are able to travel at great speed that seems to astonish your people upon Earth. They also understand the principles of 're-generation' that is the replacing of 'organs' and the structure of their bodies of light. Upon some of those planets illness as you know it has been completely eradicated, it is all done through 'harmonious thought process'. They have learned to harness and 'tame' the life giving elements that abound in the atmosphere that envelops their worlds.

So you see dear friends upon the Earth, you have such a long way to go, haven't you? Your inventions that are created so often have destructive elements within them and that is how they seem to be used. If only they would persevere with the constructive side then you would find that they would make gigantic strides in bettering the lives of those upon your planet.

You do have a lot of the necessary ingredients for this, they are there waiting to be discovered, or should we say, 're-discovered'. For a lot of what you use for one thing only has many, many different properties if you care to look for them. We know of them and we do try to influence those who are trying to unravel some of those hidden mysteries, in fact in a short while your scientific bodies will 'come up' with astonishing discoveries. BUT, and it is a big 'but', the world of big business *must not* be allowed to get their hands on them, for if they do, then all the good intentions that were started out to benefit mankind will be *priced out* of the reach of those who need it! We warn you now before it is too late. The world that you dwell upon is for *everyone*, and that means that what is created is for the *use of everyone* not for the favoured few.

Treat everyone the same then you really will create a Heaven on this Earth of yours. And how can that be brought about? By *Thought*. Yes, by *Thought*, for by thought *creation* was *created* and that is how Man can live up to what was intended by the supreme Creator. *Think before you think*. That needs thought if you are to interpret correctly what we are saying!

We started off this talk with *Thought* and so we will end it with a *thought*. That is: *LOVE*. When you think with love then you know that thought is what really matters if you want to live a life that you can be proud of, and yes, one that God can be proud of too.

Chapter 8

May 14th 2003

More Thoughts

Our previous discussion was about 'thought' and its reactions. Well, we will continue with that subject for as you are well aware, everything that one does starts out, as it were, as a 'thought' and if that thought is to be used then the result is just what you are doing now. Except that it is *our* thoughts that are in control and that are guiding your pen hand. So you see, thought power is quite a mighty tool when used properly. We did mention thoughts that come to you from 'without' that sometimes surprise you, that is because you are a 'sensitive' that is how we are able to influence your thought patterns. This procedure though when spoken about may sound complicated. In reality it is quite straightforward when the rules that govern it are used as they should be.

There are others who would use another person's thought mechanism for their own advantage and that is abusing this ability. We do *not* go down that path, for we abide by the law that pervades the whole Universe and that is the freedom of a person's willpower. It must never be tampered with by an outside influence, but permission *must* be obtained by the instrument if another being is to be allowed to influence that one's freedom of the will. It is a gift from God the Divine Creator and He alone has the right to influence a person's willpower, and no one else.

There are of course those persons who deal in the world of the occult for their own purposes, and they are transgressing the natural laws and in time they will have to answer for their conduct. Those people are of the darker side of Spirituality, for believe us there is a darker side, that is used by the unscrupulous person, not always with the intention of deceiving deliberately, they just enjoy the feeling of authority that it gives them. *But* it is wrong, and they do know it, and so eventually they must give an honest account of their actions. 'Spiritual work' is a divine work and not one to be entered into lightly. Those who are willing to be used for this work must do so with a clear conscience and indeed a desire to do the chosen work for the purpose of helping others and not just themselves. So often a soul will start out with the best of intentions and their whole aim is one of service. But oh so often they fall by the wayside and certain material advantages take over and they do, as it were, abuse that gift of spiritual sight. If only they would not go down that path which is not only a slippery one but also it is difficult to get off of! Spiritual gifts, and that is what they are, gifts bestowed by the One on High, for the purpose of helping others and not just for personal gain. When you know that you possess that gift then it is something to be cherished and guarded and only used for the enlightenment of others. For using a gift of the Spirit means that you are using a gift from *God* and so it must be used in *His name* and for *good purposes only*. So you can see dear friends upon the Earth plane, that you must never abuse that gift for though it is given, it can also be taken away.

Those who desire to be of service to Mankind have a great responsibility for they are seeking to enlighten others, and this must be achieved with *LOVE*. And when it is, then that gift is being used wisely as it is intended to be. The spiritual side of Man is the one that is the permanent one, the one that never dies, the one that is seeking the pathway back to the creative source of Life itself. The path is narrow and straight, so make sure that you remain upon it, for there are many other paths that may seem to be the easier way to return to the source of all creation, but they are false paths and only deceive the unwary soul. We are placed upon Earth to *test us* to see if we are learning the lesson of *who we are*. For we are more than this physical body that we inhabit while dwelling upon this plane of 'illusion'. For dear friends it is illusion! It is not permanent, it is not what it seems, when you begin to accept that you are more than this human shell, then you have started back on the road of spiritual growth. This is what should be taught to all who are upon this Earth plane, that man and spirit are ONE and not separate. If he learns to live with that knowledge and live *by it* then he would find that this life upon Earth would make more sense to him. For he would see it for what it is, a stepping stone that takes him back to his home, the one of the *Spirit*, the only true one. We all talk of *Spirit* as if it is the one of non-reality, when it is the human body that is that one. For the Spirit body is the only true one, the original one. The one that has always been and always will be; for Spirit is the Essence of the *One on High*. The true body of the Creator made *not flesh* but *spirit*. Flesh is but a cloak that is put on and then discarded when it is of no further use. It has served its purpose for it has opened our eyes to our potential of who we really are. So guard your Spirit jealously, for it is he who will guide you on the path back to where we all come from. Spirit is the source of all *Life* and Life is what the Spirit is all about.

So, if you are one of those who have chosen the path of service, be pure in your hearts for you are doing *Holy work*, and how you *live* influences others far more than you perhaps realise and perhaps will ever know! The gift of Spiritual knowledge is a gift to be treasured and passed on to those who are willing to accept it and who in their turn will pass it on to others, and so it will grow and grow, just like the grain of mustard seed in the parable!

We will leave you on that note.

Chapter 9

May 15th 2003

The Journey

Yes, we are going to talk to you again and yes it is going to be about those beings from the Higher Spheres of Light. You had thoughts earlier regarding 'them' and we feel that we are in a very PRIVILIGED position to be able, as it were, to introduce you to 'them', though that really is not quite correct, for you cannot personally 'meet' with those on that Higher Sphere. Even we are not in a position to do that, but we have been informed that this 'exercise' is to be a 'one off'. That is your Earth expression, is it not?

Now where to begin? You must remain passive, for though you are to undertake this journey it will be in your subconscious body and not your physical one. Nevertheless it will still be a reality, believe us. So now we take you to the very edge of the Sphere of Light and wait patiently to see what will develop. We are with you all the time, for this is a privilege for us as well as for you dear friend!

What is it that you can see?

The light is so strong that it hurts our eyes and we have to avert them until we are told that we may raise them and view what it is that is before us. We are being 'told', but that is not the correct word for it is through thought communication that we understand the words that are being imparted to us, or rather 'through us'. For the language is one that is no longer one of spoken words it is a 'feeling' of what is being conveyed, and words cannot really convey what is actually taking place. We remain silent, but we understand as you do, or will, in time of retrospect!

The 'beings' that are before us are, how can we put it? Formless, and yet they are recognisable as, no not a body, but an 'apparition' would be a better word of explanation. The 'form' is within a sphere of translucent light, that is constantly moving like a cloud of vapour that seems to swirl about and yet remains still. This vapour, though translucent, is nevertheless one that has a feeling of solidity. 'It' is oval in shape and within its 'folds' we perceive not with our eyes but with our 'senses' an outline of what we will term a 'figure'. A figure that is not as we know it, for we only perceive as it were, a 'part' here and there. Nothing tangible, but a feeling of 'eyes', a 'face' that is blurred to our sight, hands that are outstretched in a blessing and we also 'see' feet. Yet all of these 'forms' are encased as it were in this swirling luminous cloud of vapour-like substance. And from its very centre we can feel such 'Love' that it is indescribable. It is a power that envelopes us, becoming part of us, taking us to heights of pure ecstasy so that we feel intoxicated and are ready to swoon. This power of *Love* is like nothing that we have ever experienced before, we feel that we are no longer 'us' but now a part of what we are observing. We look down at ourselves and we see nothing but this vaporous substance for we are now part of what we are EXPERIENECING, and yet we know that we are only sensing this occurrence and that we have not altered. Only our perception has been heightened so that we have glimpsed what one day perhaps we shall be! We are overwhelmed and feel very humble for we know that we have been part of those from the very highest spheres of light and understanding.

These spheres that are also the coverings of vapour of our

companions tell us that they are not only who they are but they are also part of what it is that they belong to! How can we put it that it makes sense? They *are* the very fabric of the world from which they have come from! They ARE life force in its original state. They are the 'beginning' and the 'end'. They just *are*! They represent all of creation before it is created! We know that that must sound out of this world, and of course that is exactly what it is, if you can get our meaning, which we feel is quite inadequate in its interpretation of what we are perceiving and experiencing. These 'beings' of Light are not as we think they are, they are beyond description for they appear, how can we put it, a form that is of human-like appearance and yet it is not a human. We think we are given that impression so that we can identify with those in that Higher order! They also appear to us to be 'huge', if that is the right explanation. For 'huge' is the only way we can explain the feeling that they generate in us! A feeling of a 'face' seems to emerge from within the vapour's clouds. One of extraordinary beauty that shines with a light that is blinding and yet it is so tender and loving; but as soon as it appears it is gone, lost in the mist and we are left longing for its return.

We feel as if arms are enveloping our very beings. We are content, we are safe, we are *home* where we belong and where we long to be. But we know that we are not yet ready, but we have been given a glimpse of what can and will be one day! Our companions of the Light know of the AWE that THEY inspire in us and try to calm us for we are in a state that we have never been in before. A voice floats over us, it is like a wave of soft music that enters our very soul, we are calmed and peace invades us and we are content once more. The 'voice' has implied that a blessing has been bestowed upon us and it has included you dear friend for our impression was that the voice *echoed* the thought: "We welcome the little person from afar, he is a Brother in truth as you all are."

The voice is like deep, deep waves of love and sympathy and as we look, the clouds of vapour begin to lose their strength. They gradually recede into the distance and we are left with a feeling of loss and yet somehow we know that we have been blessed and have experienced what very few of us have had the privilege of receiving.

And so little Brother, we are returning you back to where you have come from. Read over carefully what has been written and know that *you* have been allowed a glimpse of those beings who dwell, not on our spheres but on the Heights of pure light and love. They are the rulers of our very souls and the keepers of our DESTINIES.

We bid you dear Brother farewell and know that you have been blessed, in very truth you have. Farewell.

Chapter 10

May 17th 2003

The After Life

So we say to you Peace dear little brother. Peace! You have thought recently what is this life all about? Many people think the same and the answer that they want to hear is "yes, it does matter, and yes there is a purpose in it all."

Sometimes it is difficult to see just what a person's life does mean to them. They think to themselves that at times it seems quite meaningless. Their lives are not spectacular, they haven't achieved anything that they feel warrants words of approbation. They just 'get on' with the day to day living and what may or may not come after that doesn't seem to be that important to them, for they do not know personally what this future existence holds for them. They may read books, go to lectures, discuss with friends what they think they know about the life to come but deep down they feel "what do I really know, what is the truth about this so-called 'after life'?"

So much has to be taken on trust doesn't it? You either have to believe what has been said, and read, or you have to dismiss it as not proven to your complete satisfaction.

We all need proof, don't we? That is when we are dwelling upon the Earth plane.

Here we *know,* for we are living proof that the so-called 'after life' does actually exist. It is *real*, it is not just wishful thinking on a person's behalf! There is proof if you want it, but so often it may be overlooked because the proof that is given is so ordinary that some people argue that what has been said to them is so general that it would apply to anyone!

But what about those little personal details that only you and your 'loved ones' know about. Things that are so ordinary that in some instances you have to be reminded of the circumstances that are being talked about. And here we are talking about clairvoyants who have that ability to commune with those who have passed through the veil that joins the two worlds or lives together. The very ordinariness of these things surely is the 'proof' that you are seeking? So why is it that so many people seem to need constant reminders of this phenomenon?

We do understand the reasons, the loss of a loved one can never be replaced while the one who is left has to go on with the living without their physical presence to comfort them. One day all this will be different for we shall no longer be, shall we say, 'parted' by that spectre we call death, for the two worlds will be more like one, though in reality *they are now*: but we are not fully aware of it!

Death, or the passing from one sphere to another, has always been one that most people do not wish to dwell upon. Yet it is a very necessary procedure if we are to go on living and learning in the world that is far more real and permanent than the one upon the Earth! Like all of Nature there is a time, a reason for living and a reason for 'sleeping' to awake to a new beginning. Whereas upon the Earth plane the trees and suchlike slumber in the Winter months only to come alive once more in the Springtime, they do not need this form of 'death' that human beings need to release the spirit within their mortal body.

With Nature the Spirit of the tree does not need a release for it is just 'sleeping', it remains where it is growing, death only comes to it by man or by natural causes. We cannot alter what is a Divine Law, the body of man can only last for a set time and then it has to be put aside to allow the Spirit within to continue its lifecycle. That is the Natural Law in motion. This body of ours is only for our use while upon the Earth, it is not, and never was, intended to be our permanent habitation. We are loaned this vehicle and we must return it when its usefulness has been exhausted!

It's a law, and if we can not only see it but also learn to accept it then perhaps this separation from one who is loved can be seen for what it is, just a temporary removal from our sight but *not* a permanent one. They, *we,* go on living, perhaps not seen by the physical eyes of the ones who are left behind, but *they see* and *know* all about those who have been left behind. They are not sad for they know that the separation is only temporary; it will *not* last, they know, and are a continuation of their life force. It cannot be quenched, it was given by *God* and in and through Him it will continue for ever.

This Earth time that we have to spend is for our own good. It is to awaken us to who we really are, here we learn about our separation from the Divine Source of all Creation, and we know of our inner desire to be part of that Divinity once more. So as we strive towards that goal we learn what it is to be parted from that Divine One by, shall we say, being parted from the one who we love upon Earth. We know that we will see God again one day and that too applies to the one we lose and cannot physically see.

But it is a certainty that we will be reunited with them the separation is but for a brief spell that may seem to last a lifetime. When you think of the term 'Eternity' you must realise that it is really only a very short period in what we know as our 'Lifetime', which does not cease just because we leave this one behind when it is time for us to continue our journey of life upon the next sphere, in our upward progress. You *never lose* a loved one, for they are forever with you in your memories, until the time comes when you can share those memories once more in reality! Believe that, for it is the *Truth*.

The bond of true love can never be broken, just as God is a part of you, you are part of the one you have given your love to as they are a part of you. So remember we part to be reunited and this time forever. There is no such thing as death for the Spirit, that is Eternal and can never, never die!

Chapter 11

May 19th 2003

Love

Much has been said about the reasons that we come to Earth to learn, and so we think, learn what? Is it how to live a fair life not upsetting anyone, or just trying to get through it as best we can?

Well of course those things are important, but unless you are aware of why certain things happen to you, lessons are not learnt are they? Mistakes? Well yes they are important to one's character building, that is if you don't keep repeating them! For if you do then there again you have not yet learnt the lesson that a mistake is trying to teach you! Viewed in that way you learn to appreciate that a mistake when properly understood can become a stepping stone on the pathway back 'home'. Nothing need be wasted, all part of what we call Life and what is it all for?

It is to equip you for what in due course awaits you in the next life! So then you think: how can that be? Surely the next life will be different to this one upon Earth?! Yes and no is the answer! You will not have the same situations to overcome, but the ones that you have mastered upon the Earth plane will have given you enough information to overcome what may turn out to be a similar situation. Our life upon the plane of the Spirit is a form of continuation of the Earth one, we are not always aware of what 'lies around the next corner'. That goes for situations as well as for the people that create them for us! For most situations that 'crop up' are to do with our relationships, aren't they? They were upon Earth and they are no different here! People don't always 'get on' with each other, that's all part of the tapestry of life! But you learn how to tolerate what you perhaps do not like and when you find out what it is that makes you incompatible with another person, you have truly learnt a valuable lesson.

But don't think that this is all there is to life upon the Spirit World! There is far more to life than just learning how to 'get on' with other people. Of course it helps if you do, which is obvious, but it is not necessarily the main answer to any problems that may arise. People are people, and that is an end to that. If they change then that means a worthwhile lesson has been learnt, but they have to 'want' to change and change for the better, it has to come from them because they know its the right way to not only live but to 'get on' with one another! But as we have said not all situations are the result of another person's actions. Though just as it was upon the Earth situations do come about because of 'people'. After all we are all living together aren't we? And that of course means that we do not always see eye to eye with each other, but that need not be a stumbling block to our associations with other people. If we learn tolerance, and of course that goes for *us* as well, for we may be somewhat of an obstacle to another person, after all perfection is a long way off even though we are striving for it! Though not necessarily being aware that that is what we are trying to do!

We have said that situations 'crop up' that need handling and overcoming, upon Earth we had to learn how to handle these situations and so we still have to here! It would seem that we cannot get away from the reasons for situations occurring and when you think about it, they all have their roots in the actions of others, don't they? So it is important that we learn how to accept what may transpire that needs our, shall we say, tolerance and understanding?!

Life is full of surprises. It always has been and it looks as if it always will be, so the main lesson, if you wish to call it that, is to learn to *Love* one another and in doing that you find life is so much more pleasant and yes, rewarding.

Now loving one another doesn't necessarily mean that you have to like another person! That might sound like a paradox, but it is a truth. If you learn to live by love, you learn to accept people as they are and not how you expect them to be! So learning to see another person's point of view makes for a more comfortable mode of life, doesn't it?

That way you have learnt how to 'get on' with people, you with them and they with you! Life then will progress and not stand still, for after all people are the main stay of a successful life and we are *not* talking about success in business! Being a successful 'human being' is what we should all aim for and that means being unselfish in all that we do, not to have to keep thinking "I must be unselfish in such and such a situation". It must just be a natural way of life, and here we are talking about whichever life you are living, whether the Earth one or the Spirit one. They are both the same, aren't they? For that is what life is all about. Though to some people it seems that it takes them many lifetimes to come to that conclusion! More's the pity! Love is the key to all of life's problems, when you have learnt the true meaning of that word then you are well on the way to living not just a good life but a *God life.* That goes for whatever sphere of existence you may be on!

For *Love,* that is the *Universal* kind, makes the worlds go round. You notice we have said *worlds,* think upon that for that is what our life is all about.

Simple really, we were born in love, the love of the Creator so if we live by that principle then we are behaving as God intends us to, shouldn't be too difficult should it?

For you can accomplish so much more with love, tolerance and understanding, than trying to get your own way in everything you do. It doesn't work in the long run believe us. It maybe a hard lesson to learn, but surely the rewards that it brings, shows that it really does work, you know it does, so why not start right now, it's never too late, for a lifetime is forever believe that. It is FOREVER!

We bid you Farewell dear friends upon the Earth and we leave you with not only our love but the Love and Blessings of the One on High! Farewell little scribe you must be getting tired!

Chapter 12

May 23rd 2003

Religion

We think that in tonight's discourse we will talk about the Religious culture that pervades the Earth plane and, yes, our plane as well. For we too have religious culture just the same as you have, only here Religion is, shall we say, more 'open' in its thoughts and behaviour. Plus the fact that in the Realm of the Spirit, 'Religion' has been 'around' for a good deal longer than it has upon Earth!

That may surprise you, but we know of many more 'cultures' than have existed upon the lower plane. We absorb, as it were, cultures from other Sphere's of existence. Here, we not only tolerate them but we analyse them as well, to see what the basic truths that they may or may not have. You naturally think that the Spirit World Religion must be of one kind and one kind only! Is it upon the Earth, dear friend, or for that matter elsewhere in the universe?! Oh yes, Religious thoughts and their subsequent 'action' are 'Universal' in every sense. People do not alter their religious beliefs just because they transfer from one plane to another! 'Religion', and that word is much maligned for it covers a multitude of misunderstood thoughts. It has been the 'bane' of so many different cultures. Each one believing that it is they who hold the key that unlocks the truth as to what and who is *God* and what are His intentions towards His offspring!

If they could only cease this searching for something that is basically so simple in its concept, and live what that means, they would be a far happier race, and that goes for all of the humanities. 'Religion' is 'man-made' not *God's*. He needs no Religious thoughts to understand His principles for right living. Mankind has obscured the simple truths with trappings that dull the senses and make the thoughts of Man mixed up with all kinds of what is termed 'mumbo jumbo', and that is not 'getting at' the practices of the coloured races. For that word aptly describes many, many so-called religious practices. And they do go back to even the beginning of time in the life of Mankind and others!

They seem to think that a simple explanation regarding *God* and His thoughts cannot be real, they think that simplicity just cannot explain what really is unexplainable. God does not require an explanation. He is what and who He is, and that is all that there is to it.

God, as you call Him, can never be fully explained in layman's terms. How could He? For He is beyond explanation and yet He does not require Man to try and explain His existence or *otherwise*! Accept the fact that *God*, as such, is beyond 'explanation', that is where Man in his search for the truth as he thinks he sees it has 'gone wrong'! *God or Gods* or the *Creator or Creators* can never be explained. They JUST are! And that is as far as we will ever know.

You may gasp at our use of the word *Gods* for *you* would like to believe in just one that you personally can identify with. That dear friend, we can never do!

However much we would like to think that God is *our* God and no one else's. It is natural that Man tries to identify himself with a Creator, but if he stops to think he would know that this is an impossibility and entirely impracticable.

There is, shall we say, an 'hierarchy' of Celestial beings that are beyond the comprehension of man and his weak intellect! 'They' are the 'keepers' of the 'worlds' that are under their, shall we say, *'jurisdiction'*. That should make you think! We call them 'celestial beings' so as not to confuse you too much, for if we call them 'gods' you would say "blasphemy" and cease to read further. But think carefully before you dismiss that statement out of hand. God, and we still use that word, is not only *ONE*, but *MANY!* That probably is too much for you to take in, and probably will continue to do so for the foreseeable future!

At one stage in Man's development he was perfectly happy to be associated with multiple God-like figures and in some countries upon Earth still is today. Old habits die hard! But they do still hold grains of truth, believe us. There are so many variations of what you term the *Truth*. Turn it around and you get another aspect that is still the Truth. It is like those weird structures in your fairgrounds, you can either see yourself as one or many; tall and thin or short and fat! But they are all *you* nevertheless! They are distortions of the original.

Think upon that and then apply that thought to your religious views! It would be better to have *none* than go on believing what you have been told is the one and only Truth. No one has that authority, believe us. We see so much error in Man's thinking, and we have to contend with it when he has departed from his Earth home and comes to us full of what we would term 'primitive ideas'. We cannot and do not try to erase them, for Man must do that for himself and believe us it takes many, many lifetimes before he is ready to accept what we can show him is the Truth. Yes dear friend, we *show* him, we do not just *tell* him. And when he is ready to accept that, then he is ready to really begin the journey back to his source, the source of all creation of which he is but a small but significant part of.

So dear friend, don't judge another person or race of people because of what they believe in. In time, *all* peoples *everywhere* will understand the simplicity of the *Truth*, no need for all the trappings that have hidden it for so long, bring it into the open and live life as the Almighty has decreed it should be lived. Do not cease your searchings little brethren of the Earth for Truth is there waiting for you to discover it. But do not be disappointed if it is not what you imagined it to be. Just remember that Truth has many disguises and it is up to you to find out which is the one that is the *True one* for believe us there is *only one* Truth and has always been and always will be!

Chapter 13

May 25th 2003

Garment's

We have watched your thoughts and though we applaud your thinking we feel that we must try to inform you about those other 'bodies' that you have enquired about in your thoughts. You are right in assuming that there are many of these 'bodies' but not all of them are necessarily used by the Soul in its search for its true identity!

You may say that these so-called 'body projections' are like a wardrobe of clothes that one has but does not always use, or in fact need. They are there because they are thought to be of use!

Now you wonder what happens to these 'bodies' or shall we say 'outer garments' for that is what they represent! Just garments that are put on *when* and *if* required by the 'owner' as it were. These garments are only for the use of the one who has fashioned them and they cannot be transferred to another 'soul'. They are *your creation* and therefore *your* property! However, they must be looked after for they are a form of living vibrating energy waiting to be put to the use on the creators behalf.

Now Soul is unaware of what these 'entities' are capable of achieving on their own. Though without the consent as it were of the creator of these other bodies they can and do remain 'inert'. You wonder then why they are created in the first place if they are not all used. They are, shall we say 'safety nets' in case they are required should anything 'go wrong'!

That surprises you no doubt, but most people are under the illusion that the whole of the Spirit Worlds are run like 'clockwork'. Not so dear friend! If they were then where would we be in the scheme of things? No, incentive to progress on our own, we would become like 'automatons', turn a key and we behave as programmed!

That is *NOT* how the Almighty has planned His creations. He has given them not only life but a will of their own to use not only for their own benefit but for the benefit of others as well! You see life on all of the various spheres of existence has *not* been planned, it is open to variations, 'mutations' if you like! For 'mutations' need not be useless, they often point the way to a better form of living matter!

We are not perfect, for that is what we set out to achieve is it not? You say: "well surely the Soul is perfect, isn't it?" Yes dear friend it is but it has no knowledge of what perfection is! That is why those 'garments' that we spoke of are necessary to its understanding of why it needs to know of its created perfection in its original state!

Soul remains upon the Soul plane, it does not leave that plane of existence, for that plane is 'perfection'. But it, shall we say, 'slumbers' until it is awakened by one of those other bodies that have been animated as living, breathing entities; learning, adapting and informing what it is that their lives are teaching them! Most people tend to think that the physical vehicle is the only one of real importance! It is *NOT* but that is not to say that it is not important in the evolutionary cycle of existence!

We start with *Soul* and then work 'down' through those other spheres of existence and learning until we reach the one at the bottom of the chain. The physical interpretation of the perfected Soul upon that upper plane of existence!

As we have pointed out, the Soul has many 'garments' to choose from in its many forms of incarnation before it can understand the meaning of perfection! I expect your head is reeling from all that is being said! Not yet though, that will come as you read over what has been imparted to you!

So we will go back to the physical you upon the Earth plane. You live, you 'die' you live again, maybe not straight away for you have much to shall we say 'put straight' before proceeding on your journey once more. Either back upon the Earth plane or if you are ready then *here* where you have come to, so often either after your leaving the Earth world or in your form of death which we call the 'deep sleep state'. Not all dreams are of importance, most are just a jumbled version of everyday living, some are memories of the past that keep recurring in different versions, but *they* are not the ones of real importance!

It is the ones of the deep sleep that we speak of. For they are the ones where you come face to face with the one who looks after your physical body while you dwell in it! You, as it were, 'take stock' of your experiences and your Spirit assesses what you have learnt and advises you as to what would be your BEST path to take, that will give you the information for you to progress.

Still *your* choice dear friend, you don't have to take the advice proffered, but you would be very foolish not to, believe us! All part of your living and learning and becoming, what you know you should be. A part of the One on High that has been manifested by His Love!

Now that is *perfection* at its highest level. To create in Love and to give to that creation the ability to choose, whether to live a *God* life or not and yet still be *loved* by the one who *created*! We have been given that God quality of *Loving* and *loving freely* for to love as *He loves* means that you do so without reservations, for in loving another person or persons you are behaving like God for in truth you are a part of Him are you not? But how often do we think like that? Sadly not as often as we should, for if we did then life would truly be wonderful to live, so that we would want it to go on forever! Heaven that you call it could start here on Earth if only people and nations had the courage to say: "Are we living how we should, how we know that God wants us to?"

It seems though that we have to leave this Earth life behind before we really start to live a God, which is a good, life and really live it and not play at it!

So you see those 'garments' that are waiting for us to 'put on' are of use, aren't they? And each one that we do 'put on' has been fashioned, as it were, by the ones that we have *left off*. We have left the most beautiful garment till the last so that when it is time for us to present ourselves to our loving Creator we can feel that we have not let Him down. He will see us as we really are, not in raiments of cloth of gold or royal purple, but of *pure white homespun* true and honest, with no pretence!

And so we leave you here. You no doubt would like to know more about these other spheres that we all have to inhabit on our way back. Well perhaps one day we will tell you, just a little at a time when you are ready!

Chapter 14

May 28th 2003

The Law!

When you think about our World of the Spirit, you conjure up all sorts of ideas as to how and what the terrain of the World of the Spirit looks like. You imagine quite a lot and some of it we have to say, is correct. But not all of it. For to each person our world remains something of an enigma as in fact we seem to be as well!

We will try to dispel some of these MISAPPREHENSIONS. We are just like you, for in truth we have been as you are now. The exception being that we are, as it were, capable of many more things than we were when upon the Earth plane! Here we not only abide by the law of Universal Brotherhood we are as it were that law! You must realise that wherever one finds oneself, in the Universe, you are governed by its law! Break it and you suffer the consequences. Look at your Earth and you can see the consequences of the breaking of that law! You may not always realise it, but actions have REPERCUSSIONS upon those around you.

If the harmony is broken then disharmony is the result. And here we are speaking in terms of Nations as well as the individual who make them up! So much of your unhappiness stems from greed, in its many forms! For greed need not necessarily be for another's gold! It can be of their Spirit. And here we speak of 'breaking it', for that is what is done in this search for conquest however much it is disguised as a form of restoration of ideals!

Ideals for whom? Not always for those who are being subjected to a form of foreign invasion! Think twice and even thrice before you embark upon THESE so-called crusades. In most cases they have a hidden agenda and that is to benefit not the oppressed population but the so-called liberators! *Laws* broken, and what is the result? You can witness it for yourselves as you are doing at this very moment. You do *not* have harmony in your world today because the basic law of 'Love Thy Neighbour' is forever being broken! That dear friends is a lesson that *must* be learnt, and practised as well if you wish to live in peace with each other.

Here upon our sphere of learning there is *harmony* and we all profit from it. That is not to say that we do not have differences, but we know how to use those so-called differences to become advantages to all concerned! We know how to tolerate each other's opinions, but they do *not* clash with one another. We have learnt to 'live and let live' and that is achieved by *Brotherly love* in all its many aspects. Brotherly love, and here we speak of the Universal kind has to be achieved, it does not come automatically just because you have the garb of the Spirit! After all, we are still *human* and we use that word to express that we are still, even if our so-called body has been changed!

Living upon this sphere that you call Spirit has many advantages, as you will find out for yourselves. We learn to live within our limitations, for there are limitations just as there are upon Earth. Though here we must stress that these limitations are somewhat flexible! That is not to say that they can be 'ignored' but you can learn to *stretch* them, as it were, providing of course that they do *NOT* impinge upon another's way of life!

You see, we *do live here*, and that means *Live*. We are not airy-fairy wraith-like beings we are, to put it into your language, 'Flesh and Blood'. Not exactly, but you understand the meaning! We are 'solid' if you wish to use that expression, and yet we have the ability and knowledge to alter that perception when it is required! All part of our learning techniques, for it does have to be learnt, believe me.

Our vibrations as you are aware are much higher and faster than yours upon the Earth plane, that is why we are able, as it were, to manipulate our surroundings and our *form of light* when we deem it is necessary! When we say "form of light" that has a different meaning to what you may think it does. For *light* is not just 'light' in the sense that you know it. It is a 'perception' of what a person is and not what they may appear to be! We *see* as it were, the one that dwells within the outward form. Yes dear friend, we too have an inner and outer body-like garment that is who we are! Just like upon the Earth. We live an 'inner' life as well as an 'outer' one. We are no different in that respect. And you are well aware of what we mean by *inner* and *outer*, we know.

What we learn from our 'outer' life is transferred as it were to our 'inner' for assessment! How else are we to progress if we do not *live* and *learn*. By which we mean that we have to not only accept what happens to us, but also we learn how to put to good use what it is that we are learning in our 'every day' living! You see, we are no different are we? And yet we are, for we know what it is that life upon our sphere is for, we do not stumble from one experience to another like you upon your plane of existence. Each time we experience a 'happening' we learn from it there and then.

So progress is continuous and does not fluctuate, like one step forward and two steps back, as it is so often the case upon Earth! That is not to say we are all goody goodies! Far from it! We are as we have said, just human beings with a different garment which we have put on while upon this sphere. No, dear friend, everything is not plain sailing as you would put it! If it were we wouldn't be learning anything from it, would we? It is all the ups and downs and uncertainties of life that make all of living worthwhile, wherever you are! We have to *work at things* just like you. We have to use our thinking powers constructively whatever the situation, by which *you* understand that we are not perfect little angels! That may surprise you, but wouldn't it be boring if we were?!

So you see dear friends, this 'lesson' that we are imparting to you is to show you that becoming a Spirit is nothing to be apprehensive about, it is a continuation of your Earth life, albeit one of higher expectation in all aspects of that life. One where you can see the results of your achievements and build upon them. So this life to come will be one of joy and yes amazement, for life really does open up for you if you are prepared to *live* it!

We bid you farewell on that note and later we will tell you more if you wish.

Chapter 15

May 29th 2003

Children in Spirit

We know of your own thoughts on the afternoon of yesterday, and so we will try to clarify what you were thinking. You wondered about children of the Spirit plane and also certain members who were as we have said before in a form of transit through our realm, waiting to return to the Earth plane when their period of rest and recuperation has ended.

First we will talk about the 'children'. Many are Souls that were to be born upon the Earth but were, shall we say, *diverted* to our plane for a particular reason. It may be because there was no suitable vehicle for them to incarnate in at that particular time, or that they themselves did not wish to visit your plane of denseness.

Well for whatever the reason they choose not to be incarnated, it is their wish and it is to be respected. Now you begin to wonder what happens to them. Well there are, as you know, upon the Spirit plane people who are partners, kindred spirits, either when upon Earth or upon the Spirit plane. They are, shall we say, suitable candidates for the Soul who does not wish to proceed further, to become a member of that family group! They choose the family and it is with *their* consent that they become one of the household.

They are now that family's sole responsibility for bringing up that child to full maturity when it is then free to choose what it then wishes to do. So you see, families here are just the same as upon Earth, with the exception that there is no biological reproduction in the sense that you understand upon Earth. The new Soul is placed within the family unit in a way that is entirely acceptable to all parties. And so a new family is created in Love and understanding, and quite often other child souls will wish to gravitate to a particular unit and so a family grows larger just the same as upon Earth. It is a great responsibility for the Father and Mother to accept and it is done with complete co-operation from all concerned.

Child Souls are true love souls and learn all about what may await them if and when they feel they may wish to incarnate upon the Earth plane at a later date. If not then they quite often remain in the Spirit realms as Higher entities with specialised work to perform.

There is of course more to all of this than what we have given to you, but you can now understand a little more of how and why it is that we have children upon our plane. Some of course are souls that have incarnated, and for various reasons not remained, upon Earth and return immediately to the Spirit world. Here, as previously stated, they become a member of a particular group, though they can still remain the child of the Earth parents and do remain in contact with them while growing up IN the Spirit world. This explanation should be able to satisfy your curiosity on the subject.

Now to proceed to those persons who have left the physical realm at death and are now awakened upon the Spirit realm. We will only deal with those who wish to return to Earth for reasons best known to themselves. *It is their choice* and one that has been carefully thought out by them after consultation with those whose work it is to guide these souls in their desire for further experience upon the lower plane. There are areas set aside for this very purpose and when the Soul feels they are ready to return to Earth they are taken to these areas for, as it were, 'schooling' to show them the various opportunities that can await them when they reincarnate!

They can and do, shall we say, 'try out' various so-called projects they can 'live out' a lifetime upon Earth in an abbreviated version and one that is, shall we say, projected at great speed, but is not noticed as such to the person concerned. These various 'projects' can be analysed by the 'player' whose life has been viewed, and they are then free to choose the one that they think will suit them for the learning that they know they need before progressing in a permanent fashion upon the Spirit world.

All of this needs a lot of careful preparation, they are shown various skills that may apply to a particular incarnation. They can and do learn them thoroughly so that when they are required upon Earth in their new life, they perhaps find a particular skill comes easily to them and they wonder why. But of course do not know that they have previously learnt that skill, so it is not a 'gift' as some might think but one that has been *earned* and *learned* and can now be put to use for not only themselves but to help others also. We all have to learn, and though some people upon Earth think that others may have things easy, it means that they have had to learn what seems to come easily to them. It is NOT a gift, it has been sheer hard work on their part, before even being re-incarnated. So do not envy another's *good fortune*, they deserve it if you did but know it! There is such a thing as justice you know, even if to some it seems obscured. There is always a reason for everything, if you care to look for it. Never judge what you do not understand and if you did understand then you would not need to judge would you?

We can't always see why things happen, but they are usually the results of past actions, be they good or bad. The art of overcoming them is to know the reason *why* and then you can go on from there. Another lesson learnt, and hopefully it will not need to be repeated! All part of living and yes, learning!

Chapter 16

January 13th 2004

Tolerance

Why do you think your world is in such a peculiar state at the moment?

There is much talk about global warming and the effect it is having upon your planet. What you are witnessing cannot be put down entirely to that phenomenon. There is much activity that is taking place not only with*in* your planet but also with*out* it! There is a great deal of 'mental upheaval' all around you and it is causing distress upon those people who are of a sensitive nature! There is uncertainty amongst the nations, nothing seems settled, nobody it seems trusts anybody these days, and we are not just talking of local affairs, but national ones!

Some of your politicians are 'coming out' with very strange utterances that are making others anxious! People are *not thinking straight*! And that goes for your world in general. They have made *gods* of power and privilege, they seek material possessions and ignore the spiritual! In fact, they do not even believe in things that they cannot touch and observe and possess! Your whole way of thinking has become *flawed*. You covet! You exploit! And you do not think of the consequences of your actions. We look down on your palaces of so-called pleasure and we are appalled at what we see. Your youth are heading rapidly for disintegration, not only of the body, but the *mind*. Those that come over to us in tragic circumstances are bewildered, unable to focus on anything that involves their mental faculties! Our places of rest and recuperation are overflowing with these tortured restless souls.

We are left to try and piece them together and believe us it is well nigh impossible in some instances! Many don't even want to be helped and if you ask them why, they cannot tell you! Many are suffering from *drugs* and we do not just speak of the obvious ones but the insidious ones of selfish greed and intolerance of other's lifestyles! There seems to be no feeling of comradeship these days, it is all ME, ME, ME! We can see that it will take a major catastrophe to bring people to their senses! And what a waste of human beings that will cause! You have 'progressed' if that is the right word far too quickly with your technological advancement and left behind the traditional values of family life!

The whole structure of the family is threatened, and for what? So-called pleasure of the senses! "Must have this". "Can't live without that!" You have lost your sense of direction. You were far happier when there was less of these material possessions that you surround yourselves with these days. You cannot take them with you when you *die* can you? You were born with nothing, and nothing is what you take with you when your life's journey is over! Do not ignore the *treasures* of the *spirit* for they are the ones that last. And that also means the ties that should bind the family together!

There is so much wealth that is squandered these days and we are not just talking in terms of money but of physical relationships that cannot be bought with finance. The currency should be *love* and we mean *universal love* as well as the personal variety.

Start with the family. Go back to some of the old values that were proven to work for all concerned and when you get stability in the family unit then that will strengthen the national one and you will begin to see the whole world beginning to come together in harmonious living. *Tolerance* is what is lacking in today's society. Tolerance of lifestyle, tolerance of ethnic origins, and tolerance of what is called *Religious Culture*! *God* sees into the *hearts* of *Man*, he sees beyond the outward show of piety and sees religious bigotry and intolerance of other people's feelings. Take a good look at yourselves and your motives before you start to criticise others' actions!

Back to that word *tolerance*. You have what you call the *Ten Commandments*, a blueprint for a good life and one that works if you give it a chance! It's still not too late to change your ways, and you will reap the benefits that will result in harmony and prosperity amongst *all nations* and *peoples*! If you can live in harmony with nature she will repay you a hundred-fold. Cease your destruction of your natural resources. Replenish your soil, plant forests, cultivate the land for food for that is what it is primarily for and not to be concreted over for high-rise buildings and car parks! You can't eat concrete but you can eat what the earth can produce when you let it!

Don't let this Earth become a *dead planet* like the ones that orbit your sun. They did have life once, but through waste and neglect they ceased to be a viable living environment! Don't make the same mistakes as they once did. We are giving you sound advice. *Take it* and make use of it, do not delay, conserve what you still have and don't exploit your resources to *destruction*! You will be the losers and no one else! And blaming someone else won't help you one little bit. You are *all* responsible for your own actions. Pool your resources, share what you have with those who have not, and in time they will repay you in like kind!

It really does work, when you work together for a common cause!

Chapter 17

January 23rd 2004

What Next?

Peace be with you dear friend. So often when we feel, shall we say, 'lost', and we think about the past and wonder about the future, we come, as it were, to a blank wall! We are brought up with a start! Where has our life brought us to and more to the point, where is it now taking us too?! So much conjecture and not very many answers to our thoughts! Life has slipped by almost without our realising it, and here we are wondering "what next?"

Well, of course, there is an answer and we know what it is. It is that sooner or later our transition will take place, and this life of ours upon the Earth plane will be just a fading memory. A lifetime of living, and the outcome of it? Just a fading memory!

And yet there must have been a reason for being upon the Earth, what was it? Was it to learn a lesson? Or rather, 'lessons' and what were they for? Surely they must have been for a purpose?

Yes they were and are! They are to prepare us for the future life upon the Spirit World, that is what we are told, isn't it? And then what? More living, more lessons, and then another form of transition awaiting us?! Does it never end?

Perhaps we are not meant to look that far ahead. One step at a time should be sufficient. But one can't help wondering and speculating about what this future life will be! Are we prepared for it? Or will it come as a surprise? Yes it probably will, for the life that we are embarking upon is nothing like the one we have just left and yet there is a lot about it that is familiar! We are now an *adult* about to start a new life, not as an infant, but a fully grown person with a lifetime's experiences behind us. A bit of a dilemma, for we don't know just what to expect, we are in a strange country and what are we going to do about it? It's not like when upon Earth you went away for a holiday and when the time was up you came back home! Back to familiar surroundings, back to normality, with pleasant memories to think about until the next holiday time arrives!

But 'here'! Well there's no going back after our visit! For this is no holiday, it is the start of a new life! And what sort of life will it be! Unfortunately, most people are ill equipped to start this new life, there's a lot of 'baggage' that they need to get rid of before they can *step out* upon this fresh pathway, that leads *where*? Such a pity that we are not told more about what this new existence is all about, when we are upon our previous one!

But then who is there to tell us? It is up to us to try and find out for ourselves, and quite frankly that's where the difficulty starts! So many variations of what people think of what awaits them in the world of the Spirit! The 'church' doesn't give us much information on the subject, does it? The word 'Heaven' crops up a lot, and *'seeing God'* is another thing we are told, but we are not really prepared for this final transition from one sphere of existence to another one are we?

It seems it is left to those in Spiritualistic circles to try and give us a more coherent picture of the life to come. They are the *link* between this world and the next and yet they are often frowned upon by the so-called orthodox religions, at least in the Western Hemisphere it seems! Other cultures seem more open minded when it comes to talking about the 'after life', but even then what they have to say on the subject is not exactly verifiable, is it?

The subject of the *life to come* should be more accessible when we are younger *not fanciful*, but seriously explained so that we are prepared mentally for what lies ahead of us, for after all we all have to make this transition, don't we? You can't put it off, it's the only real certain thing about this life upon Earth, we have got to leave it behind one day, and that's a fact!

So why all this hesitation about talking about the inevitable? If we know more about what to expect then we wouldn't be so apprehensive about what awaits us when death overtakes the mortal body, and our Spirit is then released from its bondage of the physical. That is what we really are, and that is the 'vehicle' that we are to use in this new life of ours! The more we know about our other 'body' the one of the *Spirit*, the easier it will be for us to adjust to the new life! For that is our, now permanent, one and has always been if we did but know it! The Earth one was the *temporary* one of habitation and not the other way around! Death in the gateway to the fuller life that awaits us and should be accepted as such and not shrouded in mystery and horror as is so often the case!

Look forward to this new life and not backward at the old one. It's served its purpose, it was but a stepping stone on the pathway to the fuller life of the Spirit, which is the *real one*, the only one that matters, for that's the one that is taking us back to our beginning back *home* where we belong. We have strayed from it, but we know that, that is our ultimate goal, the one that all this striving for is about. So go forward from this day in the knowledge that life does go on, it always has. It is *we* who have to change, to change our way of thinking and accept that our physical body that we need while upon the Earth plane and it is *only* a covering to house the true self, the real body, the *Spirit*, that is *Eternal* and can never die. For we are part of *God* and *God* is forever and that means we are as well! Live for today, let tomorrow take care of itself, for tomorrow may be the door that opens wide to allow you through to the life everlasting. The promised land, the Heaven that we are told is where we will be united with those we have loved and have gone on before us, but who are never really very far away. For we are *all* spirit and so we are all one *in reality*!

Chapter 18

January 28th 2004

The Force Field

Where shall we begin this night's discourse? What shall it be about?

You were thinking before you 'got up' about the electrical emanations that surround your physical body and yes are also within it, for these 'currents' are your very 'life force'.

As you are aware, everything in the Universe is governed by some form or other of electricity! It is the mainstay of all life force, both of the 'animate' and 'inanimate'. By animate we mean *you* and that is all forms of living, breathing creatures, and the Earth to which you cling to and from which you get your nourishment to exist. These are the 'animates'; the 'inanimates' are those appendages that make up part of the 'Earth's body'. For example, the rocks and the pebbles on the beach, the minerals that are sometimes found within them, that you upon Earth seem to prize and covet! *All* things have this field of electrical current around them. With human beings and the animal kingdom, the birds and fishes in fact all those 'movable' creations carry around with them this force field.

The, shall we say, 'stationary' objects retain this field. It does *not* move from them, it may give off emanations that vibrate, that can be observed by certain people, but it does not allow those 'objects' to move of their own accord. Though if they are forcibly moved without their *consent* as it were, that *force field* becomes 'torn' and you may not believe this but it does cause a certain degree of pain to that particular 'object'. The same applies to trees, plants, flowers, in fact to all living things that are removed from their place of *birth*!

Now perhaps you will be able to understand why you, that is Mankind in general, can be influenced by, shall we say, 'outside influences'. In other words the electrical emanations from another living creature and yes even from what we have termed 'those inanimate objects' that you come into contact with! You have absolutely no idea of this invisible, but very potent source of life giving energy! And what it can do to you if you are not protected! In actual fact you are protected by your own living force field that encompasses your whole body, it is a form of 'shield' that constantly vibrates, it is what is known as your 'aura' to those clairvoyants who can 'see' it! 'It' comprises of electrical vibrations. Each one part of the other, and so if 'one' is out of alignment then that upsets the whole equilibrium of the body. That is the physical vehicle that we speak of and *not* the spirit entity that is the 'real' person', that you are aware of when you have become an enlightened being, and we are speaking to those who are aware of this aspect of their true 'body' of existence.

Mankind has a long way to go before it acquires the ability to use these force fields for its own use. At present he is somewhat at 'their mercy', though don't take that too literally! You can now begin to see that there is far more to Man's 'make up' than what he thinks of as his physical body! This force field of living energy accounts for many of the so-called ills of the body.

'Ills' is perhaps a strong word to use and perhaps we should say unaccountable feelings of 'unease'. All of these electrical currents that flow throughout the human body can sometimes become overheated or overcharged and even entangled, causing upset and pain. These currents should be regulated by the brain, which in turn is governed by the *mind substance*. Sadly man does not yet realise the capabilities of this mind substance! He uses his mind in perhaps a rather haphazard way, instead of a logical extension of its true ability!

We know how to use our 'thought power' for our plane is made up of pure thought substance which we are a part of so we vibrate in unison with our surroundings which is in complete harmony. We do not have illness, for our lifestyles reflect our thoughts which we are taught how to use in a productive manner! As you will one day be shown how to, when your transition to this first plane on the upward spiral is completed! You follow what we say?! Our 'electrical impulses' are made up of 'many colours' and each colour is for a specific purpose and use! They can be amalgamated when required for different purposes, we do this by 'thought waves' which are actually observable if we wish.

Mostly they are invisible to, shall we say, the 'naked eye' but they are nevertheless 'real'. We do use our 'hands and arms' if we feel so inclined, but if something that we are doing requires a form of *strength* then thought power takes over! We are extremely practical, but we never dissipate thought power, for that all requires electrical impulse and that has to be generated by us! Even though it is in constant supply all around us if needed! We live, breathe and rest, all though 'electrical wavelengths'. Yes and even our 'food', if you like, is formed by electrical thought substance!

You will find so much of interest once you are upon this 'thought plane'. Perhaps one day you upon Earth will be in a position of being able to use 'thought manipulation' for the betterment of Mankind in general, and here we speak of physical regeneration of bodily tissue and yes even of bone and sinew! Hospitals will be just places of rest and perhaps recuperation and not for the relief of illness as you know them today! For illness, as we have told you, begins when the auric vibrations are out of alignment and by then Man will know how to keep them in order, hence no illness! There will be no need for doctors of the body, but there will be of the *mind*. For *mind* will be the substance that may require regulating at certain times! But all that is not in the foreseeable future, but it will come about one day!

We visualise that it will be when those souls who are about to be born upon Earth will have been educated here upon the Thought Plane, before starting their round of reincarnations on their upward spiral of cosmic evolution.

We feel that we have given you much to think about in this night's discussion, in future ones we will tell you about the many 'bodies of light' that go to make up your 'whole being' and where they reside until you are ready to be reunited with them!

Chapter 19

January 31st 2004

Other Planes

We will begin.

You wondered about those other 'you' that dwell upon the various spheres of existence that all comprise the so-called Spirit World! Our world in fact, and let us assure you we do *not* think of ourselves as spirits, far from it, even though we are able to do things that though normal to us, would be considered supernatural to those upon the Earth plane!

These 'other spheres' are in truth realities, but are not as you would think of as a reality! Reality upon our world is not the same as upon the lower one! Yours! Our spheres though observable can also be termed 'perceptions of the mind'! We have to leave that as it stands because it is too complicated to explain in language that you could understand!

Now regarding spheres of habitation to which facets of *you* as an entity like us 'inhabit' while you dwell upon the Earth plane! You are aware of *our* plane which is the *first* one, shall we say, 'up' from your lower one. There are many more that form the spiral of Man's evolutionary progress and we will only deal with but a few of them, namely the ones that are most pertinent to you! You know of the Soul plane and the one that adjoins it, though in itself separate from it!

We will now go 'down' to the next one of importance to you. This one is of 'Pure Light' and that also means 'Pure Life'! For on all spheres there is life and life in abundance! This one then is inhabited as it were by 'beings' of Pure Light. We say inhabited, but perhaps that is not quite correct, for these 'Beings' are from 'Higher Realms' and only 'comedown' to that sphere when they are asked to! Part of their 'duties', shall we say. For they are the guardians of the Soul! And so they have an interest in what that soul has created, which to put it on a personal basis is *YOU* in your many guises!

So this sphere that we talk of 'houses' on of your 'aspects'. Not recognisable as a being of human-like qualities! If you can go along with what we are saying! This 'aspect' is 'made up' of pure light waves. It is a form but, shall we say, 'formless' to the naked eye! Paradox, but true! These light waves provide a protective covering for 'what' resides within, awaiting the time for it to be animated into living activity by *you* when you return on your upward journey to the source of *your* creative principle, which is *your* soul essence!

This sphere like you who dwell within it, is very beautiful, but somewhat turbulent in its activity, for it is a 'life force' and a life force is always active, which we will not delve into here! So *if* you were able to observe this sphere, say from above, it would appear to be a swirling globe of opalescent light emanations, giving off, shall we say, *fingers of light* in all directions!

This life force is able to be 'used' by those 'Higher Beings' when they require it for use upon those lower planes of existence including the Earth one! These 'Higher Spirits of Light' have duties that take them all over our 'known Pathways' that encompass this world that we dwell upon, they do not *venture* beyond what is our known and accepted as our perimeter of existence! Perhaps difficult for you to understand! *You*, that is, that 'light body' that we spoke of, do play a part in all this, but we are not permitted to elaborate upon this!

We now proceed to the next plane, going down the 'chain' as it were! Now here *you* have become more recognisable as a human-like structure! You are still encased in 'light protection' which is emanated from *you* who are within the protective shield. Your sphere is one of great beauty and is known as 'The one of Silver', because it has an aura of silver light emanations, not unlike a moon, if you could see it! The whole plane has movement that is gentle and rhythmical, its vibrations give off sounds, somewhat like the sound of harp strings being plucked by invisible fingers! These sounds are not only soothing but also are regenerative when they come into contact with perhaps a nearby planet! The whole sphere has billowing clouds around and below it, while upon its surface there are mountains, lakes, foliage of all kinds, small trees, birds that 'hover' over the landscape they 'shine' like moving jewels!

There are 'people' just like yourself who are waiting for the return of their Earthbound partner or aspect, and so there is continual movement 'from below and above'. This sphere then is a form of 'halfway' house for those who are in *transit*, as it were! The atmosphere that pervades this sphere is mellow and soft and the light that forms a canopy is 'palest gold', the whole being somewhat surreal but very soothing to the unfolding of the senses!

Once again we leave that sphere and travel *down* to the next one. This one resembles what you would term like your normal one upon Earth, though it may look similar but beneath the surface it is different. For here, though there are towns, cities, villages, landscapes, oceans, lakes, in fact just like on the Earth plane but there is *no* deterioration either of buildings or foliage or of people! Here life just 'is'! Harmony reigns everywhere, and *you* are living upon this plane! This aspect of *you* is one of the ones nearest to you as you dwell upon Earth. Here you live a life, that is suitable to the *you* that you know as yourself! Your life here in a way mirrors the one upon Earth in many respects, but this aspect of *you* is a person in his own right! He knows of you and who you are, he is aware of your thoughts and habits and how your CHARACTER is forming, he even has a 'hand' in the moulding of it, for you that is the Earth one will one day be him, or perhaps he will be you!

Depending upon which of *you* feels is the right one to proceed further up the spiral of evolution! You will have your 'guides' to help you in this choice, and of course you will be shown the various options and paths that you can take. Of course, all of this will only happen *when* you have ceased you round on incarnations upon the Earth and *also* when your lives upon the lower spirit plane have ceased, though at times you will be allowed, shall we say, access to that Higher plane where you will come face to face with this other aspect of *you*! He may even visit you on the lower spirit one, as he has done while you dwelt upon the Earth plane, when in your sleep-state, and this you do remember, don't you?

Now we come to our and your plane of existence. The *first Spirit plane* above your Earth one, though still a part of it, though not always observed, but just a 'feeling' that you sometimes have and leaves you wondering! We have not dealt with some of the intermediaries that do exist alongside of the other planes. They are mainly visited in your deep sleep-state, they *are places* of reality that you can and do reside upon from time to time and probably will again when you dwell upon this plane of *thought*, for there is far more to life than you can ever dream of, at least while you are upon the dense Earth plane!

Chapter 20

February 2nd 2004

Death is Not the End

So we will start this night's conversation, and what shall it be about?

Your mind has been puzzled of late by lots of things that you have seen on your television screen regarding the stars and planets and ancient civilisations! And it started you wondering what it is all about, and by 'it' we mean Life! Well, to most people, that is those who bother to seriously think about life and what comes after, it all seems something of an enigma! To some, this life is pretty straightforward. They live life as best they can and do not think a great deal of why they are upon the Earth plane. It's all that they know about, it's their home so there's no real need to worry their heads too much. Just getting through life is quite enough to be getting on with, and what may or may not come after this one is over is something that they cannot think about!

Some people may think that's the best way of looking at life and we suppose they do have a point, but burying one's head in the sand will not make the fact that one day they will have to leave this life, will not solve anything, will it?! We must be here for a purpose, that is if you honestly think about it, but does anyone bother to tell you what that purpose is?

Well the answer to that one is, *not* really! For the majority of those who should be able to give you a coherent answer are usually vague on the subject, and here we are talking of those in the religious organisations. With perhaps the exception of those who are called Spiritualists! A word that to a lot of people makes them think of seances, perhaps weird goings on! People associate it with the Victorian era, when anything to do with the occult was in vogue! Some of the evidence was true and could be vouched for, but quite a lot was, to put it mildly, a lot of mumbo-jumbo!

Well this idea of communications with those in the Spirit world is almost as old as the world itself! Most ancient religious cultures believed in the after-life even if their ideas were somewhat fanciful, but the belief that there must be something that follows on from the death of the mortal body was to them quite natural, even though it was misunderstood! Looking at it from that perspective, Mankind hasn't advanced very far in his search for the answer to the Why are we here and where are we going to?!

So much has to be taken, shall we say, on trust. As we have said before, it's so difficult to actually verify for oneself what one is told regarding this 'life to come', and yet it is a *reality* in every sense of the word. We can personally vouch for it! But that still wouldn't convince some people! They will put it down to imagination or wishful thinking, but tell them that such and such a place is 'haunted' and would they be prepared to spend the night alone in that building, they will fight shy of the thought! They don't believe and yet they fear what to them is unknown!

If only the idea that death of the body is *not* the end of *life* but the beginning of a new one with all of the ills of the physical body a thing of the past. For it is a *truth* and one that can be verified if one accepts things to do with the occult with an open mind and not one closed because one cannot physically prove it to oneself! That is why the Spiritualist movement is a very, very valuable asset to those who are truly searching for the answers to this riddle of life and what it holds for us!

But, and here we must stress the fact, that not all those who practice the art of clairvoyance are, shall we say, genuine in their vocation! It is a *gift* and one that should be cherished and nourished for it has been given to those who are sensitive to the spiritual side of life, to be given out to those who are in need of help and *sound advice*. Sadly, it is very rarely that people want to know of the Spiritual side, they want messages of comfort from loved ones who have 'passed on'! That does have its place, but it must only be used as a *stepping stone* to a deeper understanding of that 'other life' that we all must eventually go to!

In the coming age there are to be teachers who will be able to demonstrate to those who are truly searching for answers. *Positive proof* that the Spirit life is one of reality and one that is part of *Man's physical make up*, one that is important to him in his everyday living! These 'teachers', though they won't be thought of as that, but in fact that is what they really are, will be in possession of *powers* that will astonish the populations around your globe! Bringing together whole communities that were once sceptical of the so-called unknown!

The powers that will have been given to them are for the purpose of opening up the psychic forces of the individuals, so that they will be ready for when Spirit and Man will live as *ONE* and know it! The two worlds will be interchangeable as it were, with Man's ability to dwell and live in both planes as and when he wishes!

He is to become a more *Spiritual being* in every way! By which we mean he will do *God's work*, because he knows that that is why he has been created in the first place. The vision of the *Creator*, that is the *sublime Creator*, is that *Man and God* should work in unison. Partners in the ever onward creation of new and wonderful creations of *life forms* that actually do exist even now on those Higher planes of evolvement. Waiting, as it were, to be brought *down* to the lower planes of existence to make of them *Higher ones*, so that one day *all planes* will be as one, in the

Heavens to which you at present believe await you when your transition takes place. Heaven and all that that word implies should not be a place to which one goes to at death, but should be the place that one lives upon all the time. That, dear friends, is the vision of the *future*, but that need not stop you from trying to become more spiritually oriented during this your stay on the Earth plane!

You may even be the forerunners of those spiritual beings of the future. Time as such is immaterial when one is thinking in terms of Eternity.

A hundred, a thousand, ten hundred thousand Earth years are as *nothing* when one is talking of the Eternal! *We all* have lived many, many times upon the Earth plane in our journey through life and yet we do not think of ourselves as being ancient, do we?

The spirit is eternally young. It is only the physical body that ages, withers and dies as is natural while upon this present Earth with its dense form of life matter that has to die to regenerate itself. Man has to abide by that law but only while he lives in the physical body and *his regeneration* is his becoming once more his true *Spiritual Self*!

We come from the *Divine Spiritual Essence* that pervades *all* creative life forms, and as that essence we can never *die*, we change, we mature, we go back to our source, but always we *live*, that is the gift that our creator has bestowed upon us. The gift of *life everlasting* to be part of 'Him' and be with 'Him' for evermore!

Chapter 21

February 5th 2004

The Cleansing

Children of the Earth you are witnessing changes that are somewhat confusing for you. Your weather pattern is no longer stable! You cannot with accuracy predict in advance as you would like! Your weathermen can work out on models what *should* be going to happen, and they are very surprised when it doesn't go according to plan!

There are many reasons for this, and it is mainly because of what is happening within the Earth crust. There is terrific violence going on deep within it and that is causing the disturbance without, and also it upsets the atmospheric pressure. You have noticed this past year that the *time* has actually *speeded up*. This will continue, for your world is being bombarded from above with random electrical discharges, over which you have no control!

You will also find that the *moon* is going to exert a stronger influence than she has in the past! This will inevitably affect your *tidal patterns*, your seas are becoming more turbulent, and the life that exists within them is going to rapidly disappear! That is those that we might call the 'surface variety', and you will find that fresh species will take their place, and they are coming from the *depths* of the *oceans*. Some of your coastal waters will be somewhat dangerous to those who swim in them, for many of these species have poisonous barbs that may not be noticed until too late! Much of these fishlike creatures are not edible for man! They will cause him stomach upsets which, if not treated straight away, will result in permanent paralysis of the nervous system!

These species will also *die out* and your seas will become barren of marine life! There will be volcanic eruptions below the ocean's floor which will cause certain areas of the sea to bubble and become hot which in turn will be taken up into the atmosphere causing MASSIVE disturbance in the form of what you now term *acid rain*. This will be very toxic and when it falls on the open countryside will poison the Earth and destroy vegetation!

All of these phenomena will *pass* eventually, but it will take time. This is in a way a cleansing of all of the Earth's pollution so that the Earth will be in a 'purer' state, ready for when the *New Races* will appear. This then is to be *their home* and no longer yours. Your species of mankind will have been returned to one of the many other spheres, some of them from which you originated! Long, long, long ago! In fact, before your history could be said to have been started! You are to be *assessed* as it were. Improved where necessary and after your period of rest which really means a form of *deep sleep* lasting for many of what you term *centuries*, you will be awakened upon your *New Earth*. No, not this one but another one higher in the evolutionary scale! All this, dear friends, is going to take *time* as you know it, but it has already started and cannot be *reversed*. *Go with the flow*, dear friends, that way all of this upheaval can be tolerated!

You probably think that all of what we have said to you is pure fantasy. It is *not*, it is all part of Earth's cycle of regeneration. It happens all the time, all over the various universes. That is why some of the planets and spheres that you observe appear to be dead and lifeless! They slumber that is all, though some will not be re-awakened, they will perhaps form the nucleus of a new one yet to be born! Nothing in the universe is wasted, it is all 'recycled' as you now term it!

Activity, activity, always activity. The life force of the creative system is always active in one way or another. It is never still. That is UNTIL..?! and we can go no further on that subject!

And that would seem to be a good way to bid you farewell, we leave you with much to think about, though remember this is all in the Future, and not yours, dear friends!

Chapter 22

June 12th 2003

The White Brotherhood

You have wondered in your thoughts as to how and where we live upon the Spirit plane.

Well, as you are aware, we are all different both in race and creed. But we all come together in one aspect, namely the Brotherhood of Jesus the Christ and so we are called 'The White Brotherhood'. But that really only refers to the garments that cloak us, for we are 'made up' of many races and so we are very diverse in not only our thinking but also our behaviour patterns.

Does that surprise you? When upon the Earth plane we were just as you are, ordinary people *but* with the inner desire for service to God and Mankind. As you too are, little Brother! That is what sets us apart, but not divorced from others. There are many other forms of Brotherhood. Not always going under that name, but nevertheless *all* doing the work that God in His wisdom has instructed us to do. We are *chosen* little friend, and we will leave it at that!

Our Brotherhood is not just confined to the Spirit world that adjoins the Earth plane. We are part of a vast empire of like souls that travel the whole universe. We meet, as it were, at various times to exchange not only ideas but friendships. We are a very dedicated band of souls and we are PRIVILIGED to be part of this enterprise. As you know our Order goes back for a very, very long way, even before your Earth plane was brought into existence. No, dear one, that does not mean that *we* at present are from that distant past. We, or rather many of us, are of *today* and that encompasses quite a long period of Earth time. You wonder what has become of those from the distant past? They are of the Higher band of teachers and inspirers that *roam* the entire universe and beyond. Teaching the wisdom imparted to them by the 'Holy Ones'.

So you see we are part of an ongoing organisation, if you care to call our order by that name!! For it does require a great deal of organisation, it is *not* a haphazard band of pilgrims but one of careful planning and that means taking into consideration the 'times' that we all live in.

Yes dear Brother, we are very aware of your present world and all of its difficulties, which sadly are brought about by Man's lack of understanding the basic principles of right living. Will he ever understand? The answer is *yes, he will.* But he has a long way to go before that will take place! And it will have to come from within him. Learning can be painful, but in reality it should not be, for to learn is to progress, and progress when properly applied to everyday living should result in joy and happiness all round, and not just for the few individuals who may practice it.

When universal Love and Brotherhood is properly understood, then not only your world but also the many others will benefit, even if they are not known by you upon *your* Earth plane. For you truly are *NOT* the only form of human-like beings that dwell in this your known universe and that should make you think, as we know you do. The *whole* of the Creative principle is so vast as to be incomprehensible to the mind of Earth man and yes, even to others who are, shall we say, your neighbours.

Just accept that the Creator does know what 'He' is doing even if it is beyond your complete understanding. You are *all* a part of this ongoing principle, always have been and always will be! You never *die*. You may change, shall we say, your 'appearance' but you remain *you* through all of your so-called *lives* whether upon the Earth plane or here in your understanding of the Spirit Realm. And yes even beyond those realms known and, perhaps more importantly, *unknown* but nevertheless just as real as you feel you and your world is!!

So much to learn, no wonder it takes so many lifetimes to even try to begin to fathom out the reasons for it all!

Now dear Brother you have wondered how and where we live, haven't you?

Well it is not necessarily a monastic form of existence! As we have said, we are made up of many races and cultures and, as we bring these thoughts and values 'over with us' when we depart the Earth plane, you can understand that we gravitate as it were to those areas where we find we are most compatible. That is where like minded companions dwell. Do you follow what we are saying?

Yet we *all* come together when we are required to do so. Some of us prefer the solitude of the monastic life; while others like the more outgoing form of existence!

We do have duties you know, and we also have our own private lives to live if we wish. We are very much an 'Open Order'. We move with the 'times'. We are NOT archaic in our outlook, for if we were we would not be of much use to today's society would we? So many people think that because an Order is called a Holy Order, we must all be of the same nature. Don't forget we are still 'Human Beings' even if we have moved to a Higher Vibration and maybe taken on a different garb of outward appearance.

We only change 'gradually', and not all at once! That is the wonderment of it all, sometimes we don't even realise how we have changed, just like you upon Earth. It is only when someone you have known tells you, that you realise that that is what has happened to you! It's called 'growing up', isn't it?

Just by living you change and, yes, we are fortunate that that is what 'life' is all about. That goes equally for this side of life as well as for the one you are living at the present. We aren't so different, are we? It's such a pity that people can't accept that! They think that once they have left the Earth plane and emerged once more upon the Realm of the Spirit that everything will be 'taken care of'. It all depends on *you*. You are still very much alive and there's a whole new life awaiting you, with all its ups and downs, but of a different nature to the ones that you have already experienced.

No real conflict, just acceptance and knowing how to adjust to what may come along, And remember: you are never alone here, you are always surrounded by *love* and *love* conquers all things!

Chapter 23

June 14th 2003

Light and Colour

Dear Brother we take this opportunity to discuss with you some of the thoughts that you have written down and would like answers to.

Regarding the light and colours that are so often perceived by those who say that they have had a 'near death experience'. They are quite right, the light and the colours that radiate from its source are unique to our world. You have light and warmth from your sun and the colours that you are aware of with your eyes are the colours of the prism of light that you can perceive. But there are far, far more than what you can observe, no, not upon the Earth plane, for those other colours that we observe are obscured by the denseness of your Earth vibrations; which are to us on the sluggish side! Our light and colours are *pure,* they are in no way polluted by the atmosphere that you have. Our light is all around us at all times but that is not to say that we do not experience twilight and darkness. But our darkness is not dense like yours. Ours could be compared to yours on a moonlit night; our 'shadows', as it were, are soft and not with harsh outlines as yours are.

You wonder where our light comes from? We do have what you might term a 'sun', which is not always visible but which nevertheless does pervade our skies with soft light that has a luminosity to it, and that is what creates some of our colour vibrations. Yes, dear friend, everything and everyone upon our planet, or perhaps I should say 'universe', vibrates! But not in a way that you upon Earth think. Our vibrations though higher and faster than the Earth's, are not observable ,as it were. They just 'are' and so are part of our everyday existence which we accept as normal.

We, I suppose, don't even notice the changes in the light and colour as your friends who have spoken of them do! Our sun, which is also like a 'prism', reflects all the particles in our atmosphere. This creates the variance in our colour spectrum. If you could catch a quantity of our atmosphere and put it in a dark room then you would see the effect that we speak of. You would see all the light molecules alive and vibrating in the various colours; separating and coming together creating even more colour variations, before separating again back to their own original colour!

This then is how our colours are formed. Quite normal to us, but of course to you would be considered wonderful, which of course they are. And honestly we do appreciate them, especially when at certain times our Suns are joined in harmony and create a scene which even to us is magical, the vibrations from each one intermingle with the other and then the colours and the harmonious sounds resonate through our whole world. The music of the spheres in actuality!

You notice I said 'our Suns', for we have more than one. Though not always visible at the same time, the light emanation from them is always there. That is one of the reasons for our light being so strong yet never harsh to the senses. We hope that our explanation has gone some way to answering your query?

Now 'bodily tissue' as you call it. Looks like yours, feels like yours, behaves like yours, but then is not really like yours. For ours is, shall we say, made up somewhat of illusion!

Do not be put off by that word, for illusion here can be a form of reality in every sense of the word. Reality and illusion here upon the Spirit World are both the same. To you that would seem an impossibility, but then you are 'looking at it' from a physical viewpoint and we are *NOT* physical as you are. If we were we would not be capable of doing the 'things' that we do, that to you would seem miraculous So much for you to get acclimatised to when you begin your new life here with us.

And here we are speaking of those in general and not you in particular little friend and scribe!

We are, as you have been informed before, able to assemble and then disassemble our bodies when and if we wish. So a *solid* human-like vehicle would not be able to accomplish that feat and yet, when we wish, we *are solid* and as we have said warm to the touch and able to do all that is required to perform what you would say are normal activities.

This all has to be learnt dear friends, but do not worry there are many good teachers here only too willing to assist you. We are on the whole quite normal looking and behaving we can assure you. We need to be if we are to fulfil our, shall I say, 'obligations' to each other. Our lives though different to yours are nevertheless normal to us as you will find out for yourselves. Life here is not one of 'fantasy' believe us, we are very 'down to earth', if you will pardon the expression! We are *not* endowed with magical powers, we just observe and work within the universal law that we are shown works for us all.

If Mankind learned how to work within *his* universal laws it would save him so much worry and heartache. Life would be a boon and a blessing and far less of a struggle as it is at present. He will learn in time, but he still has some way to go before that transpires, more's the pity!

Chapter 24

June 21st 2003

Religion!

Little Scribe! What can we say to you that will stimulate your thought process?

So much is only touched upon is it not, for we can only express what we have personally experienced and also there is a lot that we are not permitted to impart. We will start this talk regarding '*Religion*', a word that makes so many people, shall we say, apprehensive! They wonder what will come next when that subject is broached in public. For too many people their religious thoughts and beliefs are *their own* and they do not often wish to voice them, either because it might cause controversy or they wish what they feel on the subject to remain their private property! A great pity really, for if more people were to be open about their religious beliefs they may be pleasantly surprised at what may come out of the conversation. So many religious beliefs or cultures have far more in common than otherwise! If only people would look for a common denominator and not try to find confrontation either in expressing their thoughts or try to defend something that to many is quite unexplainable in ordinary terms.

What do all religions have in common?
GOD!
So surely that is a good starting point, is it not? So often religion

when talked about, or rather more often *argued* about, does not start where it should and that is the *Godhead*. They start talking about everything else that goes to make up *their* religious culture and the word *God* is just a word that seems to 'crop up' every now and again in the conversation!

They talk of the 'services' and the various trappings that go to make up those services. The 'dos and don'ts' that seem to be part of it, and the, shall we say, rewards or not that result in a persons behaviour patterns regarding their religious teachings. Somewhat like the 'carrot and the stick' that is supposed to egg a donkey on when all else has failed!

Are you donkeys that need that form of stimuli? Why do you think you've been given a brain? And a thinking machine? You have to work 'things' out for yourself and come to a conclusion that is *right* for *you* and no other.

So much of so-called Religious culture is based upon *fear*. Fear of what might happen to you if you think for yourself and not accept what has been put before you by, shall we say, 'orthodox teaching'.

Religion originally was manmade by so-called *priests* and not for the benefit of the layman, but to keep him under a form of control lest he find out for himself, what truth really is and then question the dictates of those in authority. We will not be specific on any one particular religion, you yourselves must do that! But blind obedience to that authority is not what *God* wants of you. Though remember that if you take away something it may leave a vacuum, so be sure that what you have to put in it's place is what *you* need, and not what someone else thinks you need!

You are your own judge and jury. Seek the wisdom of the *Silent Prayer*. You will receive the correct answer *when* you are ready for it. Religion, if one has to have one, should be a stepping stone along the pathway back to the source of all inspiration, namely the one you choose to call *God*; as good a name as any that tries to explain the unexplainable!

Man has always sought to try and explain to himself what he feels is part of his *inner-self*, his Spirit if you like. He wants to identify with that other body for he feels that that is the one to which he really belongs and the one that does *not* die as the mortal body has to before that Spiritual one can be liberated from its prison that we call Earth. And yet it is *not* really a prison, is it? A training ground that we all need in our discovering of who we really are. You are *Spirit* as *God is*! You are a part of *Him* as *He* is a part of you. That really is *all* that you need to know and accept as a *fact* and a *truth*. You do *not* need all those different explanations of who the Divine Creator is. Just accept that '*He Is What He says He is*'! And you are part of his wonderful creation. Believe in the *ONE GOD*, whatever name you wish to call Him. Makes no difference to 'Him'. He is *ONE* and yet He is *MANY*! We can never really understand. We may one day, and then we will know who we are, for we are part of all *Creation* and the *Creator*!!!

Look no further than yourself. All the answers that you need are within *you* for they come from the Creator Himself and were given to you from the very beginning as part of the gift of eternal life.

We *never die. Change yes*! But life goes on forever in many different forms!

So we say to you dear friends and fellow travellers, you are your own *Religion*. Live as you know how you should. Let others see what your *inner faith* does for you. No need to explain what so-called denomination you belong to, for we all belong to the same one. And that is *Our God,* our *Father*. Our *Mother*. Our *Brother*. Our *Sister*. *Ourselves* in fact!

Chapter 25

June 21st 2003

Other Identities

Well little Brother, where shall we begin? You ask about the Spirit world that we belong to, and yes *you* as well, and is it the only one that affects your known world? Well dear friend. The Spirit World as it is known to those upon the Earth plane is *not* what you think of as 'Heaven', a word made up by Man to satisfy his longing for somewhere beyond this, his Earth home. He thinks he wants a form of 'Paradise' where he is looked after from morn till night and to wish for something makes it materialise to satisfy those wants!!

We have to say, '*Grow Up*', and we do not mean that unkindly! But if he did stop to think (which he does not!) he would know that that sort of Heaven would soon pall and he would be looking for somewhere else!

As we have told you before Our and your Spirit World is a 'working world'. We are not idle and neither is this the Heaven you have been promised. No, we know that you are not personally disillusioned by that remark, but many will be.

Your Spirit World is a form of extension from the earth one, though many would say tis the other way around!

Be that as it may, the Spirit world is but one of many that you will dwell upon on your journey back 'home'. Now 'they' can be called 'Heavens' if you wish, for each realm is 'Higher' than the last, as you in turn 'become'. And so each 'Heaven' expands your perception of what these lives are for.

Now here we will tell you that your other 'bodies', a very loose term but never mind, it at least gives you a term of reference doesn't it? Well upon each of these other Heavens *'you'* are dwelling and learning. No, not the physical you which is only that replica that is suitable for the earth plane, but your Spiritual counterparts that all go to make up the one you, that you term 'Soul'; which is the Divine spark created from the Divine Creator you call *God*.

We need all of these various bodies, or rather light substances of inner perception, to enable us to eventually know *who we really are* and why we are who we are and what is the purpose for us being who we think we are!!

So now you wonder about these other *You*. They are *identities* in their own right, but they are still *you*, make no mistake about that. All go to make up the true one that you are.

Now you have wondered what would happen if you were to 'meet' as it were one of these other you!

Well dear friend and brother, you did, did you not, in one of your dream states? You were surprised and yet though he/you looked different you knew he was you didn't you? Just a fleeting glimpse but it did leave an impression upon you, didn't it? These other 'worlds' or Heavens to which these *other you* belong are all for the edification of the *Soul you* that does not ever leave the *Soul plane,* shall we say, 'in person'.

That is the reason for these other light substances that dwell upon the lower spheres which are in fact *Heavens* in *their* own right. So you see dear friend, you do go to Heaven. In fact you are there already, only *you* do not know it yet! All part of this complex form of 'life' or should we say 'lives'. That is more appropriate I think!

It did occur to you that in previous incarnations, when you took on the guise of another person, do those *'you'* still exist as a memory creation? The answer is *yes,* they do, but *only* in a form of abstract memory. They can be 'conjured up', if so desired, like a cinematograph film, for nothing is lost. You can view yourself, as it were, as you once were; and dare we say it, *warts and all!*

You may not like what you see, but it is all a form of education so it will not be wasted. You can, and some people do, 'parade' all of those other you *together* and so you can see how you have progressed over the centuries.

That may give you a shock. But it will only be your ego that is deflated and you soon get over that!

There is so much more to life isn't there? And all very interesting when viewed in perspective!

We know that you would like to know what these other Heavens are like. Do they resemble Earth in any way or are they *out of this world* so to speak?

You could not begin to understand, even if we had the words to convey to you just a fraction of what living upon a Heavenly world is truly like. *You* do know because *you* already exist upon them, don't you?

Just accept that one day this little physical you will know all that there is to know for you will be there as your 'light self' with the knowledge of what you now seek, but which has to be withheld from you in your present stage of evolution. Patience is what is needed little friend, you do know and understand far more than most of your contemporaries so be content with that explanation for the time being.

Chapter 26

June 25th 2003

Which World is Real?

And what will our talk be about you wonder?

Most things that we have said to you in the past have dealt mainly with certain aspects to do with our world the one you like to call Spirit. The *real World*. In fact yours, though real to you, is one that when you leave it you tend to forget it almost completely. It seems like a dream world when you think about it and sometimes you wonder if it really did exist outside of your imagination!

So much for the three score years and ten that so much is written about. *We* think in terms of 'eternity' knowing that as we move from one realm or sphere to another our life force is one of continuation. No break, just a fresh awareness of our new surroundings. We, shall we say, 'go to sleep' to awaken still in the same 'light body' but with a heightened awareness of where we are. Something like when you leave your Earth body behind and find yourself in your new, though somewhat familiar, light body that you call Spirit!

'Body' is such a loose term to call your new vehicle, for though it can resemble a 'body' it is not 'made up' of the same substance as your previous one. You have no need of that gross and heavy body that you have been accustomed to. That is why your freedom of movement and thought is so exhilarating to those who have just passed the transition period and are now on their semi-permanent home.

You notice we have said 'semi-permanent', that should give you a clue as to what we are going to say next!

Some will wish to remain here while others will know that for their own evolution they must return to earth after a period of rest and recuperation. And so not all persons are, shall we say, in the same 'areas' of environment. Those who are going to remain for a set period have much to get used to: assimilating fresh ideas, leaving behind some of the old ones, but not all of them, for some will be quite useful in dealing with various circumstances that will arise. Then there are those whose home this is to be for the foreseeable future and they have much to learn about this new and exciting new world of theirs. To begin to fit them for the next round of *lives* and *living them*.

We do not stagnate here dear friends. Our 'work' does not permit it! And who would want to be forever doing nothing in particular? It might seem inviting for a time but you would soon tire of it! Progress has to be 'worked at', it doesn't just present itself to you. So you see this life here is one of not only enjoyment but also of learning. And in fact learning can be a form of enjoyment when viewed properly. Those who are shall we say just 'passing through' before returning to Earth once more, have a different lifestyle altogether. More 'relaxed' as it were. Nothing is hurried and they are shown various forms of what the coming lifestyle back on Earth will be available to them. It will not be fanciful, it will have a serious motive behind all the information that is presented to them. They are not pressured in any way, they are allowed to 'take their time' before coming to a binding decision, for it is a great responsibility to embark once more upon a new lifestyle that is to help them in their evolutionary progress. They will *not* be alone when the time comes for that journey back to Earth. They will have made 'friends' with those who will be what you term 'Guardian Angels' and 'guides'. Without realising that it is those friends who will be watching over them in their coming life pattern.

You see dear friends, there is such a lot of 'going on' on our side, isn't there? Life really is worth living when you learn how to view it properly. Wherever you may find yourself! So it's a good time to start thinking about your future while you are still dwelling upon the Earth plane; that way you maybe able to minimise your future journeys back and forth.

Think about it, for ultimately it is all up to you how you wish to progress, isn't it? We can only advise and show you various alternatives but you must make the final choice. We feel that that is a good point upon which to bring this talk to a close!

Chapter 27

June 26th 2003

The Higher Beings of Light

Y ou have spoken about the other 'Heavens'.
What are they like? Do they resemble the Earth plane at
all? And also 'who' dwell upon them? Are they 'us' from the
Earth world on our way back or are 'they' entirely of a different
light form of Spiritual entity?

Well Dear Brother, what a lot of questions to be dealt with all in
one go!

First and foremost, regarding what these Heavenly places look
like. Well each one as it gets 'Higher' takes on a more ethereal look
and form. It is still 'solid' if you wish to call it that, and yet there
is somewhat a feeling about them of not quite being what they
seem!

You could say that they appear different to each individual
according to their 'progression' and inner perception. They have a
translucent aspect, almost like a 'dream state'. The light and
colours are as one if you can understand that. Colour is light and
light in its natural state is colourless, and so it 'takes on' whatever
colour is present in the 'atmosphere' so to speak. And this varies
according to the thoughts of those who are, shall we say, in
'authority'!

Thoughts and prayers on these Higher realms are all *one* and these *prayers* are *thoughts* of *positive results*. In other words they are 'creations' of a purely spiritual nature to do with that particular realm. But they are also used for realms below that one if so desired and in the process they eventually 'filter down' to your Earth plane. Somewhat 'diffused' so as to be acceptable to those upon that lower plane who are receptive to Higher thoughts. They are the *positive* reactions to the so-called *negative* outpourings that sometimes penetrate your lower vibrationary atmosphere.

You must think about that carefully and see if you can come to the correct conclusion! We can tell you that a lot of your destructive elements that seem to beset your world do not stem from it, but from 'outside' of it. There is, what you might say, a dark cloud of apathy that hovers above your known world and, where it can, it penetrates where it finds an opening!

These tears in the envelope that surrounds your earth have to be sealed and that is part of the work that certain Angelic forces endeavour to do.

We will leave that there!

You now wish to know about 'those' who dwell upon the Higher Planes that you call Heaven. Those on the very Higher ones are somewhat unknown to us on the lower planes of existence. We know that they exist and that they are not as we are, for their thoughts are so lofty that their light emanations are beyond our poor descriptive powers! Let us just say that if you can visualise a rainbow hue of a thousand light colours you would not even be near to describing their beauty.

'They' have always been there and do not venture down to the other spheres, though they are aware of the needs of these lower spheres and do send down rays of Spiritual light thoughts which benefit those who dwell upon the lower spheres.

Now on those 'lower spheres', and that word 'lower' really does not express what those spheres are, for they are so much Higher than you can really imagine! They too are peopled by Angelic forces. And do not think that we speak of Angels with wings, that's just Man's visions of what he terms Angels!

'They' are Highly evolved Souls that they have once been upon the lower planes and so understand all the shortcomings of earth-bound man. For in truth they were once that form of being. This is one of the Heavens that Man gravitates to in his upward journey of the Soul. And when he reaches this one he has come a long way in his journeying and so he might well be 'unrecognisable' as a physical entity. No longer *manlike* but *pure spirit essence*. Still his own identity, but somewhat different, if you can understand!

'Heavens' are still training grounds, for we have a long way to go on our way back to the source of all Creation!

We all change in appearance as it were. No longer needing our gross-like body and yet we are still what you can call identifiable as who we were upon Earth.

We go back to your first question: are Heavens like the earth plane?

Yes and *no* is the answer!

We will stress the similarities such as trees, flowers, animals, birds. They are in abundance but so much more beautiful than the Earthbound variety. Trees give off a fragrance that is unique. It pervades the air and is some form of nourishment if you wish it. The 'colours' are not basically green as yours are. Here they vary in colour with the form of fragrance that they exude! But they all blend with each other.

Nothing of a harsh nature exists. Flowers are so different, they not only smell but they also give off a 'sound' rather like the sound of a harp-like instrument, very faint but nevertheless audible. When a breeze caresses them you actually hear heavenly music which is very soothing and melodious. Birds and animals seem to understand the thoughts of people and respond with thoughts of their own which people understand also. It is a form of non-verbal communication. Easily understood and used constantly!

Thought plays such an important role in communication on *all* Spirit realms, so there is no way of misunderstanding what is being 'said'. Speech as such is used just as frequently as thought but is not actually necessary to communication between persons.

We feel we have answered your thought questions dear Brother, at least we hope we have!

Chapter 28

June 2nd 2003

Love is the Answer

Many thoughts have crossed your mind recently and we shall endeavour to give you an insight into what you think of is mystery, but which in fact is quite normal as far as we are concerned.

You wanted to know about the various groups of people upon our plane of light. You wondered about those that you might wish to call are somewhat antagonistic to our way of life and also our way of thinking.

Most people if you were to ask them would consider the Spirit World as almost a playground with precious little actual work for them to do. Well dear friends upon the Earth let us quickly disillusion you regarding those thoughts! This world is NO playground! *We,* and that would mean *YOU,* eventually are here to not only learn but also to be of service to those who, shall we say, are wandering around not only with their eyes closed but with their thoughts in a muddle.

Yes we have said 'muddle' for that is how it appears to us! They have not thought straight for many, many years upon the Earth plane and so they bring those still muddled thoughts with them when their transition is complete.

There is a vast area set aside for these souls who, it must be said, through perhaps no fault of their own are not yet ready to actively take up their new lifestyle upon the plane of the Spirit.

They have to be re-educated, as it were, without them really realising it. We proceed very cautiously, never in any hurry for time is of no importance to them. The groups shall we say are 'separated' almost like different 'classrooms' as you have upon Earth.

There is what you might call a 'fast stream' for some who, though needing to be re-adjusted, are more willing to accept our philosophy. These souls can be brought into the community quite quickly and can then proceed with their 'normal' life.

Others need far more serious attention. We have, shall we say, a one to one system, where that soul can as it were get all of their old inhibitions 'off their chest'. And when they have succeeded in doing that, then we can begin to show them perhaps the error of their ways!

Once they have begun to understand that the life they have led has brought them to this stage and are willing to accept what we are teaching them, then progress is quite rapid. They go up to a higher form of education, so to speak. And our teachers are very gratified at the outcome.

Then there are others who are shall we say the 'Hard Core'. They just don't want to know what we have to say. They really are difficult to persuade that their whole way of thinking *must* change if they wish to progress and be part of the mainstream of the population. Some do, and some *do not*. A lot of hard work on our part, I can assure you. If they are what we might call a 'hopeless case', they are referred to a specialist unit far, far away from the normal routine of everyday existence. In time, most of these tortured souls, for that is what they are, do come round to *our* way of thinking. But there are some, a minority I grant you, that just don't seem to want to become what most people want to be. We *never* desert them but sometimes they are, shall we say, 'put to sleep' for a set period. Complete rest, *no thoughts at all* are allowed to pass into their sleep state.

This period may be short or of a period that you would term 'years'. When they are 'awakened', we start all over again as if they are a new subject. It seems that the rest period has had a good effect upon them for most respond as we hoped they would. And so begins the slow process back to what we would term 'normality'.

Now there are those who are able to *fool us* , and they are the dangerous ones. For once they are back in the community they pose a threat to its stability! Only a threat, and *not* a positive reaction. But they are nevertheless a concern to us, for they appear to be just like everyone else and their secret desires are very well camouflaged. So you see dear friends you may come across one such person and, if and when you do, just be on your guard. You will instinctively know that 'something' is wrong. Don't feel that *you* may be able to change them! It needs a very, very strong-willed person to do that. So leave well alone! Often they give up what seems a hopeless task and so they go back to where they 'feel at home'. An area that has been designated for them and which only those of a very High Spiritual Order deign to go in an attempt to try and help even those who perhaps don't deserve it. There is always hope and so they are not deserted, and we have had some quite remarkable results.

So you see, life here need not always be quite as straightforward as you thought!

We have been talking about a minority of cases and most 'ordinary folk' will not encounter a troublesome spirit but, just like the Earth plane, you do not 'get on' with everyone. You still have your 'likes' and 'dislikes', but here you find it much easier to live with the latter for you learn to be tolerant in all things and believe us, it does work! Those who perhaps you started off not liking can, in 'time', become firm friends and all because you have learnt tolerance, which is another facet of that wonderful word called *LOVE*!

You have wondered about all those other 'areas' that we mentioned. All areas are part of the 'whole' but not all areas are, shall we say, 'available' to the ordinary folk.

You will get to know of them, for many are for 'specialist teaching'. By which we mean not only for the Spirit body but for those who are to return to the Earth plane once more and who need a lot of re-adjusting before they embark once more upon that dense planet of instruction.

You see there is so much more to our particular world than most people ever imagine. Life is very full and active here. Everyone has an aptitude for something or other and all they need is someone who can bring that aptitude to the fore. We have so many *teachers* in all fields, though they may *not* appear as the run-of-the-mill teacher class. Teaching can just be a form of *example living* without the 'pupil' realising it!

We have very subtle ways of conveying what we wish to impart. And we choose very many different 'subjects', and here we are referring to people, *not lessons*, to facilitate us in our form of education of those who want to know more of what *life* has to offer them. And here we are speaking of the life of the Spirit, the only true one. The one that lasts forever!

This world of ours is just a stepping stone that leads to the Higher Realms, where we must all go to eventually. Each Heaven, if you wish to call each realm by that name is more beautiful than the last and here we stress that 'beautiful' encompasses many, many aspects and does not always mean the surrounding where one is dwelling. Think upon that, dear friends. As has been said many times: "Beauty is in the eye of the beholder". A very worthwhile thought if you care to *really think about it*!

Chapter 29

July 2nd 2003

Learning

As you are aware, our world is basically like your own: towns, cities, continents, rivers, oceans, mountains, in fact your world in reverse shall we say. So you can see you would feel at home, wouldn't you?

Well each area or continent or land mass has its own way of life.

We do not conform to one lifestyle and so you will find plenty of other forms to excite and intrigue you if you so desire! We will tell you about the academic side, there are very large universities where those people who so wish it can continue their interrupted education from the Earth plane. There is so much for you to learn about, not only regarding your previous existence upon Earth, but also about your new homeland and others as well.

You may think to yourself, "why should I want to know about my previous world when I have just left it behind?' Well dear friends, here you will get a different perspective on the lifestyles from all over your planet which, when they are properly explained to you, will give you an insight as to how others have developed and are *still doing so*.

Think upon that! Just because you have left the Earth behind, doesn't mean that it hasn't left an indelible mark upon you, especially regarding other peoples and nations. Here you will be shown in cinematographic form how they lived and how it affected their views regarding other nationalities. You actually *become one of them* for a brief span and so you can then understand their behaviour patterns more fully.

And why, you begin to wonder?

Well we all bring over with us thoughts and actions from our previous existence. That is what makes us *who we are*!

So as we begin to progress, those previous behaviour patterns need to be adjusted. But that does not happen overnight, so to speak. Do you see where we are taking you to?

In the course of your life upon the Spirit realm you will encounter people of other races, some who you have never before been associated with. Well with your new educational studies you will understand them better for, like you, they will still be undergoing their new change of lifestyle. You will be surprised at how much you resemble each other, especially in your thinking!

So you see dear friends, life really does 'go on'. Nothing is wasted, just that the perception is altered. When you visit these other countries you will be better understood, as they will be to you.

That is just one aspect of the learning zone if you wish to pursue it. All countries have their own universities and their form of teaching will be available to you if you wish. So you see they all complement each other.

Other universities will specialise in other activities so you will have a wide choice to choose from if you so desire. You wonder why these courses are used and for what purpose. Well you may be returning to Earth again one day if it is applicable to your evolutionary progress. Also you will be able to 'help' others who are still upon the Earth plane, if that is what you would like to do. You can influence their thoughts when you have been taught how to, and so *your learning* will benefit another person, won't it? There are so many forms of learning that are open to you, especially if you have an aptitude for a particular subject, be it academic, inventiveness, art, nursing. In fact anything that you care to name.

Learning not only inspires *you* but in the learning you can inspire others. Here age is no barrier. *You are who you are*, as long as you have the willingness to progress at whatever pace suits *you*. There is no form of competition just the desire to do your best, for that is what being *alive* is all about!

You will have the opportunity to expand your whole thought patterns, for as we have told you before, here *thought* is the basic structure of everything that exists. To *think* is to *be* and to *be* is to act, and act in a positive manner for the benefit of not only oneself but all others as well!

'Learning' is a way of life, it always has been hasn't it, even when you dwelt upon the Earth plane. So do not think that the word 'learning' means that you are forever having to prove yourself, either to yourself or to others. Learning is just another word for living, isn't it? And living here upon the Spirit World is one of joy. Joy in knowing that you are getting to know yourself as you really are, the one who deep down you always felt you were.

Look forward to your life to come, the one you leave behind is but a pale substitute for the real one that lies ahead of you. So much for you to enjoy, dear friends, in every way. For *this life* really is the *real* one. Prepare yourselves mentally for the transition so that when it does come there will be no regrets at leaving the Earth one behind, for a new round of experiences await you. Life really will begin for you in earnest, believe that and know that it is the truth that we speak.

Chapter 30

July 4th 2003

Trial and Error

Thoughts about the World of the Spirit!

So many people have these thoughts and wonder if what they think is anything like the reality. Difficult for us to say *this* or *that* is the correct assumption, for to each individual what was a fact for one, is naught to another!

And so whatever we say to you, and here we refer to those in general, you must sift through what is given to you, and if you find that you cannot agree with what has been said or written, then so be it. You have a brain and a thinking apparatus and it is up to *you* to find the answer that best suits your present thinking capacity. But please do *not* discard what you do not perhaps at present agree with. 'File it' shall we say, and then perhaps at a future date take it out, give it a dust, and who knows, you might find that you already have an answer to a present question that is vexing you. That way *we all* learn, 'trial and error', the only real way to progress. So when we give to you what is in our thoughts, just remember what we have previously said. *Think for yourself* and know that what you have been given is from *our personal* point of view and we are *not* infallible!

Sorry to disillusion you if you thought just because we are Spirit we automatically become all wise and knowledgeable Far from it, for we too are *learners* as well as *teachers*!

We know that to many people the Spirit World conjures up thoughts of perhaps weird and wonderful happenings. But in reality our lives are what you might say *very normal*. At least to us they are. To you, if you were able to experience them for yourselves, you probably would consider them wonderful and hopefully *not* weird!

We all work within the *Universal Law* that affects *our* plane of existence. You upon Earth have your laws and when you learn to abide by them then life is harmonious, is it not? And here we are speaking of not only the *laws of the land*, but those of the inner Spirit consciousness.

When those are properly understood and *lived by* then you will find that life is so rewarding in every way. As it is with us!

We really are no different to you, we still think about life and where it is leading us to. Surprises you, no doubt, that we have our thoughts of *why* and *what for*. We don't possess all of the answers to the mystery of life. We gradually learn and as we previously stated through 'trial and error'. The only real teacher! We would love to tell you that all of your doubts and fears about the Spirit world are all in the mind. But the reality is that life here goes on much the same as it did upon the Earth plane. *But,* and it is a big *but*, we know how to *cope* with it.

Though everything is not straightforward, it is nevertheless able to be overcome, so do not think that the Spirit life is a form of battleground like the Earth one. We can see 'things' for what they are, and there is *always* someone who can give you a helping hand and you don't have to ask for it. It is already known. Unlike those upon Earth, who see but do nothing about it. When you have become adjusted to the Spirit way of life you will find that what may have seemed important once, no longer is. You adapt, you learn, and you go forward.

We never look back and what *might have been*. We live for the 'day' though *day* is not the right word, for *our day* is *not* like yours! Something for you to look forward to! Time here is just relative.

You use it as you wish. Difficult for you to understand but it is a fact.

Thought and *time* are interchangeable! How can we explain it to you that will make sense to you? Well, suppose that you and we are speaking in Earth terms, well suppose that you had arranged to be somewhere at a certain time and, because of unseen circumstances, you were delayed. When you arrived at your destination, the person who was waiting would wonder what had happened. But with thought transference of both parties, time lapse would be eliminated and so you would have arrived at your rendezvous at the right time and there would be no memory of the loss of it.

That will make you think I'm sure! Just one of the 'things' that go to make the sphere of learning an exciting place to be. There are many other experiences that would no doubt amaze you *if* you were able to use your present facilities to experience them. Travel, movement, being in two places at the same time, *creating* by *thought waves*, all perfectly normal activities to us *when* we have learnt how to use our powers that the Spirit is heir to. All within our Universal Law. One day upon the Earth plane there may be similar activities available, but that really is in the far off distant future!

You have in your books words that talk of 'time travel'. Well that is a reality, believe us! *But* it *cannot* alter what has *been* or what is *to be*. The laws on that subject are immutable and cannot be allowed to be tampered with. If you wish to indulge in this pass-time of time travel there are places where you can 'enrol' for these 'learning journeys'. You are guided. You can't just 'go' back and forth on your own. That could prove disastrous to the individual! But not to those who you would encounter! You are *not* observed by those others even though *you* can experience the effects of the conditions of that particular era, be it back or forward!

I expect that will intrigue a lot of people. It is very instructive and gives you an insight not only of past civilisations but of those yet to come and, believe me, they are so advanced you become astounded. Here we are talking of other planets not known to Earth Man and yet they do exist.

Regarding the Earth's future.

We are *NOT* allowed to impart the destiny of that planet, but we can say that all of the forebodings that have been prophesised are *not* necessarily inevitable! Man does have a say in his own future if he is wise enough to accept the advice that is being *sent down to him from the Higher realms. Act upon* it, for it is for his own good and those that will follow him.

Chapter 31

July 9th 2003

Religion!

Religion.
But where to begin?
We look down and see so many so-called Religious cultures that it bewilders us. We do not see what you may see, for you see only the outward displays. We see what goes on inside those thoughts that create these societies and cults that seem to spring up like mushrooms, and you know what happens to you if you pick up what you think is a harmless mushroom. It may look like the others, but the taste is poisonous and can eventually kill you!

Do you follow what we are saying? What appears harmless on the surface, once you break it open you find putrefication! So many of these cults and sects that abound upon your Earth today are not founded in truth. Far from it. Quite often they are the figments of someone's fertile imagination! They may believe, quite sincerely at first, that what they are offering is an alternative to so-called orthodox teaching, which in itself needs to be completely overhauled if it is to make any sense to the present day searchers after the truth.

The 'main' religious teachings were right for their times. But time does not stand still, it is forever on the move and that is what is wrong with the mainstream religions, hence this desire by others to try and 'fill in' the loopholes as it were. But what do they accomplish? Chaos! Yes chaos! And that is in the minds of the adherents of a particular sect.

Some seem to go back to so-called Pagan times, as even your Christianity did. It took from the rituals and adapted them so that the unwary thought that they were being given unvarnished Truths when, in reality, they were a botched up cacophony of past thoughts of a so-called Priesthood, that were only interested in subduing the gullible population who were searching for answers to questions that, to be honest, were at that time unanswerable and, yes, even in today's multi-cultural society where religious beliefs fall over themselves in their haste for converts. They want to snatch them from their so-called tried and tested cultures (which are flawed from the start!) and bring these unwary souls to their way of thinking and practising. As we have stressed before, better 'No Religion' than all of these outdated ideas of what God is all about! 'He' does not change, and within each and every one of you He has given you the true ability to not only think for yourselves but to act upon those thoughts! You must *not* accept *all* that is given to you in the name of the 'Almighty'. If you feel that what is being taught is not wholly for you, then have the honesty to question it, even if it is only in your own mind!

Sometimes to voice these doubts to others can cause disharmony. Keep your counsel to yourselves until you are sure of the reception that you will get if you give voice to your doubts. The multitude of sects that abound at this time will *not* last, for they do not contain Truths that can stand up to scrutiny. They answer questions with questions that contain ambiguous statements designed to confuse.

So many people feel that if they do not pay lip service to one or other of these religious cultures they will either be lost or, in an old fashioned word, damned!

No one is damned for not believing. Do you really think your

God is like that? If you do, then you haven't learnt much in your searching for the truth have you? *No* religion should be built upon *fear* for if it is, it will not last. Eventually it will crumble, especially in today's permissive society. Which we consider a disaster in the making! Man does need guidelines to show him how to live in harmony, not only with himself but with his fellow Brothers and Sisters. Though we were born through and in *God's love*, to human beings it does not seem to come naturally does it? You have to 'work at it' so to speak. And here we are talking of *Universal Love* which is, or should be, the lasting kind not the type that blows hot and cold as is so often the case with Earthbound Mankind. We know from experience just how *Universal Love* can work for everyone when practised with *Love*.

Actually *love* in its broadest sense could be called *Religion* if you must have a definition of that word!

Put aside what you have been told in the past, in that your particular brand of Religion holds all the Truths that will eventually get you into Heaven! No one *Religion* has that *golden key*. Though we feel we ought to say that there is always a grain of truth in those precepts that you were taught, just learn how to sift the wheat from the chaff. God sees into your *heart* and not in the catechism that you may espouse.

God is Universal. He does not *belong* to any one Religion, *He is Religion*! Believe in Him and that is all you need to help you to live a life that is pleasing to him and yourself.

So we end this little talk on Religion and say *think for yourselves,* and in the thinking ask *God* to guide you and He will, for He resides within each and everyone everywhere. And we do mean *everywhere*, for that encompasses not just your Earth plane but all of the others that people the Universe!

Chapter 32

July 12th 2003

Leisure!

Little Brother, welcome.
We see you where you are enjoying the warmth of the sun.
Actually we do not *see* you as a physical being we see, or rather sense, you as a 'light body' and that word 'body' is not correct, for we see the aura that surrounds you and we sense what you feel and think. Hence we are able to say that you are enjoying the warmth of the sun. Not seen but nevertheless observed, if you can understand that statement!

A thought crossed your mind that this interlude was very pleasant and you wondered if we upon the Spirit plane were able to enjoy a similar experience? Well yes we can and do. We are not 'working' all the time you know! Leisure activities play quite a large part in our lives here. Not perhaps the sort that you have upon Earth, but we do have our gatherings for certain sporting activities!

You are no doubt surprised at that. But as we have stressed before, we are no different to you fundamentally. Physically, *yes*! And so certain functions that you take for granted we either do not need or require in our advanced lifestyle.

You wonder what we mean by 'sporting activities'. Well for one thing we do indulge in swimming. And contrary to what you may have been told we do get wet. And, I must say, enjoy the sensation!

But, when we emerge from the water, all we do is 'shake ourselves', just like your dogs do on the Earth plane, and we are then immediately 'dry'. The children love the sea and its many diverting pleasures, they can float upon it very easily, there is never any thought of harm coming to them. We have small 'craft' and we indulge in races with them, when the breeze is in the right direction! If no breeze we use a form of paddle or oar, which we manipulate with thought power. Not everyone can do this properly, it takes some getting used to, but if you persevere you can get a lot of enjoyment in the movement of the little craft.

What else? Well we have a form of flying. No, not just bodies floating around in the air, that would never do! We have a balloon-like structure that is propelled by energy from our suns. There again it has to be learned how to do this and it's not to everyone's taste. It may surprise you, but not everyone likes 'heights' and though no 'physical' harm could come to them if anything went 'wrong' it could cause a form of shock to their 'system'. For remember we are 'made up' of very fine electrical 'waves' and molecules, and these can on occasion be out of sequence as it were, and that could cause a feeling of unease.

We do have a form of horse racing but not in the competitive way that you have on Earth. No gambling! You can have your choices and in some cases people have been known to shall we say, gamble an 'object' that they have no further use for. Oh yes, we do have possessions of a sort But nothing that is not indispensable. We have long been over that stage! People do have favourite objects, but they are *not* possessions in the way that they are viewed upon Earth. For remember we can use our thought process to 'create' and we leave it at that!

You see little Brother, so much you will find here on the Spirit realm that is familiar, we are not backward in our lifestyles. We 'move with the times' so to speak! People upon Earth have some very funny notions regarding life upon the Spirit World. Of course we are different, but then we are not so different after all. We have more freedom and more choice, granted, but we do live within certain laws and shall we say restrictions. But all for our own good, believe me!

There are places to visit that would give you great pleasure. Gardens and parks, forms of 'nature reserves' and bird sanctuaries. *No cages are needed.* Birds seem to have an innate sense of where they belong, they form groups, which do intermingle and so you see a great deal of variety in the colour of their plumage! Wild animals are no longer wild in the sense that they are predators, but they do not just roam about at will. They have their places and keep to them. They do not pose a threat to people but they are *not pets* and must be treated with the respect they deserve.

So you can see that life here is not all work and no play. We live a comparatively normal life, not your form of normal, but *ours.*

We hope we have been able to enlighten you somewhat regarding our leisure time. For, as the saying goes, "All work and no play makes Jack a dull boy"

Very, very true!!

Chapter 33

July 13th 2003

Seek and Search

All through the ages that is in the recorded history of this planet, Man has sought an explanation of not only why he is here, but more importantly where does he *go to* when he leaves this World of his. For he knows that with the death of his physical body, where does the spark that has been the guiding force go to? The part that he has not been able to verify but knows instinctively that there is 'something' else besides this physical exterior, but 'what'? He has always sought an explanation that can satisfy not only his curiosity but also that other part of him that he suspects does exist, but just where, is the problem?

Man has tended to think that if this other part is of a Spiritual nature and presumably looks like him, where is it? It can't be part of his physical body for there's no room left in it to accommodate another body-like substance. That is assuming that this Spirit body takes up the same space as his physical one. So if it is that important to him where does it 'live' so to speak?

In the past Man believed that when he physically died, he would then go to what he thought was his Heaven-Land, wherever that might be! Not his physical body, for he could see that could not be feasible. Seeing so much death around him, and the consequent disintegration of the left behind 'carcass', he felt that this other part of him must be the one that goes to this Heaven. And if that was the case then this 'other one' must have all of the thoughts and attributes of the one left behind. But he was still at a loss as to where this so-called Heaven that he was going to was!

The priesthood, or rather those who thought they were priests and had the monopoly of knowledge about this other 'place', kept the layman in his place with all sorts of explanations as to not only where he was going to but what was required of him to get there. Obedience to the teachings of the Temple or Church authorities. Plus of course a suitable contribution that would enable the priests to smooth the way for the departed soul!

Well at least that has changed in this day and age, *or has it*?

The so-called Orthodox Religious cultures do not actually tell you very much about the life and the world to come, do they?

They say 'Heaven' and leave you to wonder just what it is like and where. You are not supposed to question, are you? The scriptures, or the equivalent doctrines of all faiths, are very ambiguous when you try to pin them down about this 'after life' and it is left to those who pursue the Spiritualist way of life to come up with feasible answers. And even they are looked upon with some trepidation by the hierarchy of the Church! Yet have they any right to say that those who try to give a rational explanation of the Spirit world are wrong in their beliefs? Many of the non-Western civilisations believe in the Spirit Realm and some even have constant communication with those who dwell upon the Higher realms.

But there is still so much that we do not know or understand about the life to come. I think that what puts people 'off' from delving too deeply is all of the *hocus-pocus* and *mumbo-jumbo* that the media of today seem to wish to perpetuate. It sells papers and gets extra viewing on the television. But to my mind it is not treated in the serious way that it warrants!

A great pity, for there are many people today who are genuinely searching for answers, yes the young included, but here, those who profess to know more about what comes after the death of the body, must be careful in what they advocate. For these 'young minds' are impressionable and can so easily be misled by those persons who really are not truly Spiritually oriented in what they are teaching and doing.

You do *not* want to end up with a future population so mixed up in their thinking that chaos will be the inevitable outcome. *God* is the only one *Truth* that they need to seek.

The teachings of that one who travelled upon this Earth two or more thousand years ago are still relevant to today's society. That is the original teachings of that one, and not the ones handed down in the so-called Gospels. That is not to say that they misrepresented what had been said, but so much was *their version*, so read *between the lines* and you may be surprised at what you find! Gems of truth, advice to the seeker who is earnestly seeking and not just giving lip service to what they have read and quite often not really understood.

There is Truth in all of the *Great* and *tested religions*. Search them all, and you will find so much that is similar, that you may be forgiven for thinking "I've heard of all this before", you have! For real *Truth* is *Universal,* it does not matter in what language it is voiced. The *truth* is the *truth,* and if you are open minded you will know it when it is shown to you, whoever you are and wherever you are. And remember, Truth is not confined to this *world alone.* Or even, dare we say it, to this *Universe* as well!

Think about that for *Truth* is a living thing, for it can change your whole life, if you apply it to your way of living.

Remember also that Truth has many sides to it, it is only when you have, shall we say, *come full circle* in your search for it, that you really will be able to say "*I know the Truth*" for I have been shown it by a *Master!*

Chapter 34

July 13th 2003

Work

You may recall in a previous discourse we dealt with the leisure activities of those upon the Spirit plane of existence. Well of course there is the other side to living and that is 'working'. Not what some people would like to hear, for they seem to think that the Spirit World (if there is one!) according to some is one of continuous joy and pleasurable activity.

Would you really like it to be like that? When all through your Earth life you have been actively employed in one way or another, I expect you think: "Well then don't we deserve a respite from all of that?"

Yes you do, and you do get a form of respite. Almost like a holiday but, as upon Earth, holidays do come to an end and it's back once more to the normal routine. It's no different here, my friends. There is 'work' and there is 'leisure', a form of living that you have become used to, isn't it? So in actual fact you soon slip into shall we call it a familiar routine. But with a profound difference.

Here work activity is entirely voluntary and there is no financial incentive to do it. That is going to put some people off for a start, but there is plenty of 'time' for them to 'come round' to this new and yes rewarding lifestyle. Well now you will ask, "What is this rewarding lifestyle you talk about?"

It is *your* desire for worthwhile work activity. All through your Earth life you have worked at something or other, haven't you? You have acquired skills and why should they be put to waste when with adaptation they can if *you* wish it prove very beneficial while you tarry upon this planet. Or perhaps you had an ambition that sadly never saw the light of day, well here it can.

And what is more, if you are willing, what you now learn can be used for someone still upon the Earth plane who maybe is finding it difficult like you did to fulfil it.

Do you see where we are leading you? When you have been taught *how* and if you are agreeable you will be permitted to once more be in contact with the Earth plane but in a Spiritual capacity. You will be shown how you can influence the thought waves of a particular person upon Earth. Not to 'take over' as it were, but able to infiltrate your thought pattern upon theirs and in doing so they will 'come up' with this thought and wonder why they never thought of it before! You won't receive any thanks, but then you didn't do it for that. Your 'reward,' shall we say, is knowing and seeing how that person has been able to overcome the stumbling block that was holding them back.

You may very well be in charge as it were of quite a circle of people who will all profit from your guidance. This will not happen straight away. One at a time to start with, and your Spirit instructor will always be on hand to help you out if a difficulty arises. You will still have your own life to lead, you will not be on continual 'beck and call'. You will learn how to adapt very quickly and if you are part of a family unit upon the Spirit plane it will not suffer because of your work activity.

This is just one aspect of the life to come upon the realm of the Spirit. There are many such work activities that are available to those willing to be of service either to those upon the Spirit world or 'elsewhere'. We have an area that is put aside especially for the unfortunate children who have been traumatised in one way or another. Those who look after these tortured souls are very, very dedicated people. Mainly those who have been in the nursing profession while upon Earth: doctors, nurses, surgeons, psychiatrists and those who are known as carers and foster parents.

The area is one of great beauty and tranquillity. Nothing to jar the senses, for here the whole 'body' is taken care of. The mind has to be carefully adjusted with subtle thought. Upon a soul who has not only seen but also been part of dreadful actions which leave a scar upon the psyche and the Spirit personality.

So much love and tenderness is extended towards them. Some of the children have never experienced love and kindness, they are wary of anyone who shows it to them, but gradually, little by little, they come to accept that the love and kindness shown to them is genuine and do *not* expect something in return. These young souls sometimes express a desire to go back to the Earth plane to offer help to those still in the same position as they were. They are allowed to, but an adult helper always accompanies them, for when they return to scenes of horror they still need a form of counselling and someone they can turn to for support.

There are cases, especially those from the African continent, where they want to return to their previous parents. This can take the form of re-incarnation, or for the Spirit Soul to become a guardian angel to a member of their previous household, perhaps a brother or sister, and they truly *do make* a difference to that one's life. There is a bond that the physical child is unaware of but feels somehow 'safe'. One day perhaps this hatred of other tribes will disappear and they will realise that they are Brothers, all as *good as each other*. We can foresee the time when those of a different colour and race *will be* accepted on equal terms with those races of light skins who at present think of themselves as being God's gift to all of Mankind! If they only knew! For if they do not change their attitudes and way of thinking towards others, there will come a time when it is *they* who will be looked upon as *outsiders* and yes, pitied for their lack of accepting that *all of the humanities* are from the one Father, the Creator of all that there is.

Upon the Spirit Realm there is no such distinction. We all accept each other for what we are, for we see below the surface if you can really understand what we mean! Colour is a wonderful thing, it shows the diversity of *God's creative ability*. Looked at that way, you have no need to be antagonistic to those whose colour is not the same as your own. For believe me colour is everywhere in the Realms of the Almighty and that word encompasses much.

There we feel that that is quite enough for this discourse. There is so much more for you to find out about, not only *us* but yourselves as well! So we will bid you a farewell and hope that you have learnt something from these pages.

Chapter 35

July 15th /16th 2003

Other Areas

What is so intriguing about the 'after life' the one you call the Spirit world?

Well of course that *is* the one that we all eventually have to go to isn't it? So of course like any place or foreign country that we intend to go to, we try and find out as much as we can all about it. The good points and the bad ones. Though we assume that there can't possibly be any 'bad points' to do with the world of the Spirit! Are we right in that assumption or is there a remote possibility that somewhere there does lurk what we term 'bad' points?

Well let us try and put your mind at ease. If there are any bad points or perhaps we should say 'places' that exist, are they a threat to the everyday existence of the inhabitants? The answer is an affirmative *NO*. But these places or areas *do* exist. And though not generally known about, it would be wrong for us to ignore the question These areas or places are kept strictly apart, they do not impinge upon what we will term the everyday living cycle of most people.

The reason that these places do exist is because they are inhabited by those souls, or should we say 'wayward Spirits' that have brought over with them all of the unpleasant thoughts and vibrations that they acquired when upon Earth. These have to be systematically eliminated before we can even start to re-adjust these souls to what we term a normal 'life cycle'.

Those who do this 'administrating' are very strong willed people who have been taught how to handle these wayward souls. It needs not only patience but also an objective point of view. They, that is the administrators, *never* get emotionally involved with their subjects. However cunning and manipulative they happen to be!

You see their whole lives have been spent in cheating and lying their way through that life, and it hasn't ended just because they have left the earth body behind. They carry over all of the evil thoughts that have been accumulated. So you can understand why it is that those who are going to try to rehabilitate these souls have to be themselves not only strong willed but also extremely strong 'characters' in combating these evil streaks. Though in some cases, when one of these tortured souls really repent of their past misdemeanours and are genuinely determined with their efforts of recovery, they *can* and *do* make excellent administrators eventually, for they fully understand why 'things' went wrong in the first place and they know from this experience how to help their fellow sufferers.

So you see, we do not 'give up' on anyone and believe me our success rate is extremely high, and we are very proud of our achievements, especially when we can rehabilitate them into society once more

Well now you know of perhaps what you might call the 'darker side' of the Spirit world. Though please remember that the *light and love of God does prevail everywhere.*

Well now that you have been informed about the 'bad points' let us lift the veil on those that are good, and yes do predominate believe us, and they are the areas where the majority of spirit persons dwell.

Our cities, towns, and yes, hamlets all have a place in the lives of us upon the Spirit realm and believe me our buildings are not just fanciful edifices conjured up by someone with imaginative ideas. They are solid and permanent. As permanent as we wish them to be! We have architects and planners just as you have upon Earth. Does that surprise you?

Building has to be properly organised and approved of. There are those who have always been associated with the building trade and wish to continue with their chosen profession. We do not have what you would term 'bricks and mortar'. Our buildings are first thought of and then a blueprint is presented to those who are in authority, once approved of then the work can begin. You probably have visions of buildings suddenly coming into life overnight as it were. No dear friends, we are not magicians, we work within the boundaries of our laws and limitations. Our form of, what you might call, *building blocks* are created by *thought* and are permanent. Everything is planned to the last detail, though it is possible if during the construction plans need adjusting they can be very easily and do not cause disruption. Our builders are very skilled in their craftsmanship and often visit other sites or even countries to further their ideas and so you get a wonderful amalgamation of different styles and yet all blending in with each other.

There are numerous parks and gardens in the cities and towns for people to relax in and come together for social gatherings. You see life here really is very similar to your previous one, isn't it? Concerts, artistic enterprises, galleries and yes even a form of cinematograph entertainment, which really is nothing like your Earth variety, for here you are a part of what you are viewing if you wish. Difficult to explain, but it is quite rewarding as well as entertaining!

People often gather in the parks in the evening for 'open air concerts' and seeing friends and relations for there is much to talk about and discuss. When music is being played you actually become part of what you are listening to. It seems to envelope your whole being and you feel not only uplifted but also refreshed in a spiritual fashion.

There are what you upon Earth call 'excursions' to various parts of our world where you can see how others live and progress, for just as upon Earth we are not all the same. Neither is our lifestyle, and yet we all live in a form of harmony, for we are all living in *God's Love and His Bounty*!

So much for you to look forward to; and not only to renew old friendships from previous sojourns upon the Spirit World. It is like coming home from a long stay away. Things you have forgotten about but soon 'pick up' again. Some of these friends may even be anticipating returning to the Earth plane for a further period, and so are anxious to find out the state of the world that they are returning to. Reunions and also partings, all part of life, are they not? Remember that here, thought is all important in everything you do so learn, or perhaps re-learn, how to use it constructively so that it is a benefit to one and all.

We have only been able to give you a glimpse of some of the things that await you. Perhaps at a later date we will be able to further enlighten you regarding this next phase in your upward journey of life.

Chapter 36

July 17th 2003

The Godhead

You have been thinking of late, what is it all about? And by 'it' we mean life, life upon the Earth and why is it that it seems necessary that we have to sojourn upon that lower planet when there are so many higher ones that beckon you. How can it be that the dense planet of Earth can be so important that we all, at one time or another, have to incarnate upon it. And believe us incarnation does not mean just once, but many, many times when we have to be, as it were, alienated from the Godhead and all that He stands for?

You would think, wouldn't you, that one lifetime away from the Almighty would be quite long enough for anyone. But dear friends, one lifetime or a dozen, or more, still does *not* fit us to be in the presence of that one on High. And even when these incarnations upon lower Earth have run their course and we are back upon the realms of Spirit, we still have a long way to go before we reach our goal, and is that not feasible if you think about it? For the Almighty, the Creator of all Creation is nothing like we can ever imagine. Artists down the ages have tried to portray what in their minds they think that their God is like. But 'He' is nothing that resembles the portrayals that these artists have put upon canvass! 'He', the Creator cannot be put into a human like category. There are no words or efforts that can capture what the almighty embodies, He is beyond it all and that is how it will remain! We are allowed glimpses of His creations that are a part of Him, you, me. All of the humanities, the earth the sky, the unknown Universe and beyond, how could we poor mortals and Spirits that we are ever aspire to be in the presence of that Divine Unknowable One? Let us be content to bask in the sunlight of His love, viewing all of His creations with wonder and yes astonishment, and knowing that *we* are part of that Divine Creation. Our minds just cannot begin to understand all the complexities that go into the creation of just one of the vast creations that we see all around us. So one, two, or a thousand lifetimes just cannot justify us into thinking that we are all worthy of ever reaching that Godhead. *And yet!* Because of His love for *all* of His creations, He allows us to visualise what it is that we think *He is*! Even when our thoughts fall short of the actuality of that *Divine Force,* for *Force it is.* Not as we know or think of as *Force,* for the *Life Force* that emanates from the One on High can never be measured in a degree that would satisfy us. How can it when that *Life Force* is what sustains us through all of our lives, and that Force is *LOVE*, the love of the Creator for His Creations! And that does not just mean Mankind! *Everything* that *is,* is sustained through His *Love* and because of it. Look around you, the grass, the trees, the plants and yes even the ants that hurry about on their daily tasks! Marvel at what you see and then feel humble knowing that you too are part, just a small part, of all of this wonderment that we call life.

We are, we are told, created in *His likeness.* The Father *of* and *to* us *all!* That is what He has allowed us to understand so that we can, in our own way, identify with Him. For as a human being that is how we are able to come to terms with what really and truly is *unknowable* to us, just one of His many and varied creations. That is the measure of *His love* for did He not allow Jesus the one who was His emissary upon Earth to show that through *His Love He*

Identifies with us? He knows our failings. He knows just what we are capable of, the Highs and Lows and yet still *His love* sustains us and never wavers. We are a part of that Divine Creator, why do we not try to emulate Him?

We are shown the way and yes we still are, the Christ Spirit is all around us and yes within us also. Your Christs' have always been visible if you have the eyes to see them and the ears to understand what they are saying. Follow their example, they are not Saints, as you think of them, they are your fellow human beings that allow the love of God to shine through them and so enrich the lives that come into contact with them. Look around you and you will see that the neighbour who is your neighbour could be the one that could one day be seen as the Christ Spirit that you knew but did not *know*!

Go on searching dear friends, for your lifetimes upon Earth and beyond are your gateways to eternity. We all travel the same path and one day we will all be together in that Heaven of Heavens, knowing who we are and why it has taken us such a long time to accept that we are not only a part of the One on High but can it be that we *are* that One on High! That was made manifest in order to know who we really are.

We will leave you here and know that the Love of God is all around you and in you, so share it with others, who in their turn will share it with you. It goes on and on and is never ending believe that for it is true.

Chapter 37

July 5th 2003

The Mind!

We have observed your thoughts upon the written pages and so we are here to enlighten you somewhat regarding those thoughts.

It would seem that you tend to think of the 'mind', the instigator of *all* thought, that it is some sort of substance that you could perhaps hold in the palm of your hand! Well in actual fact you could. But it would be so small that it could easily get lost in one of the many lines that criss-cross your palm.

Now that *will* make you think I'm sure! For the 'mind' is such a complex mechanism that it almost defies description At one end of the scale it can be smaller that a 'micro dot' and at the other end you won't believe it but it can be enormous like nothing you have ever seen before.

Now of course that needs explaining doesn't it, if it is to make any sense to you. 'Mind' is a creation of the Almighty for the purpose of allowing the Soul to find out for itself its 'true self'. It can only do this by manifesting upon the lower planes of existence, the Earth one included. 'Mind' leaves the Soul and proceeds on its downward path creating as it does numerous 'bodies' that it may need in its progress back and forth! These bodies or 'light forces' belong only to the Soul, even though it may not be aware of them at first! The *mind*, which is the creator of *all* thought manifestations, is entirely in control of all of its creations. Whether used or not!

As you are aware Thought is the mainstay of the Realm of the Spirit. That is the Universal Thought we speak of and not those of the individual. Though of course they do play an important part in the overall structure of our planet. More of that later!

Mind, when it is in the body of the mortal man, is somewhat restricted in its behaviour. It can only influence the brain of man, for all of his living purposes. That is its function when it is in the human body. But when that body dies, it is liberated and can then, in its Spirit body, become what it really is! A creator of seen creations. As you know even upon the Earth plane everything stems from Thought. It is that which carries you through life from beginning to the end. Thought comes into everything we do. It has to, for that is its prime purpose in its evolutionary progress of all of its satellite bodies of existence. So you see the *mind* is more than just important, it is the very life force of Man's existence upon the Earth and elsewhere!

When as we have said the Earth body dies and the mind is liberated from it, it then takes over completely the Spirit body. It has been, in part, dwelling within it, or rather an aspect of the mind force for it is able to, shall we say, split itself into little 'segments' that can do the work that it is programmed to do. Now once upon the Spirit Realm it can give itself full reign to its possibilities. Not only animating the Spirit body, but also creating what it feels that body needs or requires for its journey on the upward path. Now you begin to wonder just what is this Mind like if it is so small and yet so large that it can be such a dynamic force! It is the thought element of the mind that is the outward show of its wonderful properties. For it is the same essence that the Almighty is 'made of'. It is the Creative principle of all Creation! Nothing can be created unless it is thought that is the mover in its creation.

So you see we are little gods in our own right, aren't we? As you know from your own inventors, everything that can be invented can be made smaller and yet retain all of its original concepts. So just imagine what a wonderful creation 'Mind' is, to be so small and yet be able to become whatever it desires. Large or small makes no difference to the outcome. 'Mind', that gift from God, that very part of Him that He has allowed us to use and use wisely and for the purpose that He intended!

We now come to *your version* of the 'Spirit body'.

It has some original thought we must say and you are on the right track regarding the substance that you think is within the body, but it is *not* correct! We are, shall we say, 'made of' what you might think of as a 'jelly-like substance'. That can become hard and yet it can also be made 'fluid' when we wish. That is with 'Thought once again'.

We vibrate as you know at a much higher rate than the physical body and so if we wish and are able to manifest ourselves to you on the physical plane we would lower our vibrations to match yours. But if in the process we wished to become as it were invisible to you, we would only need to higher those vibrations and our body would become transparent and so not observed by you, and yet we could remain where we are even though not visible to you! That is just an explanation of what we can do when required.

Also, your objects of solidity we find no effort in 'going through them'. For we can see right through them to the other side and so, to us, they are transparent, and are no obstacle to us, even though to you they remain solid. It's all to do with the 'vibrationary force', we can use it as we wish and so objects of solidity are as nothing to us! Yet on the Spirit Realm we all appear to each other as solid beings, we do not use our powers of transformation unless the occasion arises when it would be wise to do so.

As we have said we are a sort of jelly-like substance that can be altered if we wish to do so. From solidity to fluidity in an instant. So to the observer we would be and then we would 'Not be'! We could then if we wish be somewhere else, and then become once more solid.

All very strange to you, but once here you are instructed in the ways of the Spirit and you soon get used to using the powers within you for sensible use and not just for the so-called 'fun of it'. Though we must admit that when a newly arrived individual is shown how to use these powers, they do try out all sorts of actions, and we are very patient and understanding and know that they will soon tire of this new plaything!

Chapter 38

July 19th 2003

Think for Yourself

Why is it that those who seek to know more about the World of the Spirit are rather preoccupied with, (how can we put it without causing upset?), what we consider rather mundane things! They want to know how their loved ones are. Are they happy, and if they have 'met up' with so-and-so?

Dear friends, your loved ones have lives of their own to be getting on with, so much that was relevant while they dwelt upon the Earth plane seems of no importance whatsoever. They have moved on while you that is you upon the earth plane have, shall we say, 'stood still', at least mentally if not physically. You see dear friends, we are trying to tell you in a kind way that so much of what *you* remember about the life that has passed is of no consequence to those who are on the upward path of knowledge. Earth life has ceased to be relevant to them, that is why so often those left upon the Earth plane seek to enquire of those who have 'gone on' and are disappointed when a particular loved one never seems to be able to be contacted by a clairvoyant medium. We hesitate to say that they have more important things to do than to hover around the Earth plane, but that is the truth! Those who you seem to be able to contact relatively easily is because they have not yet decided to progress beyond the first stage upon which all newly arrived souls find themselves.

There are many reasons for this, and most of them are of a personal nature. They may have left unfinished tasks upon Earth, or they may have a strong Karmic-like link that prohibits their moving on so to speak, and yes there are many other reasons that we do not wish to dwell upon!

Life upon the Spirit plane is one that is being *lived* by those who inhabit it. There are 'degrees', shall we say, of where those who either wish to progress further or who are entitled to be upon other spheres of this world in their upward progression. You see, dear friends, we all progress at different 'rates' and so even members of the same family may not always be together. That is not to say that they cannot be. It is just a question of where and when it is suitable for their reunions. Try not to look at this from an Earth bound viewpoint, for if you do, you will be bound to be disappointed and even upset. But you needn't be, for everything has to be taken into consideration and we can assure you that 'justice', if that is the correct word, is always *'just'*!

What we are trying to explain to you is that how you have been upon Earth reflects where you will be in the Next World. We can never alter what has been, but when we are upon the Spirit World we start out 'afresh', as it were, and so if you really wish to be part of your previous family unit there is no reason why in time you cannot be. Though we can tell you that not every family unit from this your recent past is necessarily the unit to which you 'really belong'.

You must think about that, for if you are a believer in re-incarnation you will understand what we have said. Just remember that here in the Spirit World your whole perception is 'heightened'. You see things as they really are, and not how perhaps you have imagined them to be! Relations with people alter as you progress, thoughts are different and so are your reactions.

You are 'growing up' as it were. But do not be disheartened, Karmic ties are very strong especially those of what we shall call a loving nature'.

The other kind can be overcome and 'nullified' if you have the wish and the courage to do so! Think upon that and do remember that you will view things differently here, they are not the same as upon Earth. You have progressed, for the mere fact that you have left your Earthly body behind is testament to that fact. You can begin to alter your way of thinking while you are still in the Earth body, that way progress comes that much easier, when you start out again on this plane of enlightenment!

Try looking at things from a different viewpoint, look beneath the surface and we are not just speaking of individuals but the whole of your lifestyle and yes beyond, if you get our meaning.

Those of you who are the thinkers must have your feet firmly on the ground when it comes to discussing matters that you like to call 'Spiritual'. People do tend to get 'carried' away somewhat and believe what they want to believe and perhaps not what they *should believe. Think* for yourselves and do not let someone else do the thinking for you, for you will be getting their *thoughts,* and while it may be quite right for them, it may not be the same for you.

Remember dear friends, the Spirit world is a world of 'reality' it is *not* a *fantasy* world. We are far more practical in everything we do and think than we ever were when dwelling upon the lower sphere. Be level headed in your thinking and if you do not agree with what we have said we shan't mind, for after all *you* are *you* and have a right to your own opinions. And in time you will be able to judge for yourselves whether what we have said is the truth or not!

We feel that this is a good place to end this discussion, even if it has been rather one-sided! But we hope that it will stimulate you into taking a different perspective point of view and perhaps finding out things that so far have not been on your agenda.

Chapter 39

July 22nd 2003

Bring Back God

Individuals upon the Earth plane often wonder how they can make a difference to the lives of those who dwell upon that plane. They think to themselves "Why me?" "I'm no one in particular, so how can I make a difference?"

Dear Brother, one does not have to be spectacular to make a difference. Only very, very rarely does that happen. It is the gentle drip, drip, drip that wears away the stone, not the cascade of water that rushes over it and leaves it dry once more! In other words, *you* that is *all* of *you* are only required to be what we will term *yourself*. It is by example that the message of the One on High reaches most people and that, let us hasten to add, is perhaps not even realised by the majority of people!

You are not expected to make Earth shattering differences to the everyday life of those around you, but just being an open-minded God-loving person, that is all that is needed. In today's society, when change is looked upon as the requisite mode of living, those of you who can by their own example of stability, show that change is not always needed, for the old tried and tested methods have proved in the past to be the right way, the way that really does get results!

And yet some will say, change is for the better, but we say to you, change just for the sake of change is not the best way forward.

Look around you and you can see for yourself what so-called change is doing to society. People want to feel *safe* and change makes them feel just the opposite. Change can be acceptable if it is done gradually and not in a hurried fashion leaving behind large *gaps* that need some form of filling up! And with what? The older generations look upon today's youth with apprehension, and we can understand why, for the youth of today do not know where they are going! They are like rudderless ships that are tossed one way and then another, at the mercy of the fickle winds of desire.

Roots in the past must *not* be pulled out, for when they are there is nothing tangible to replace them. Before you seek to do that you must be sure that what does replace them is based on *Truth* and *fact*. Young people of today seek only the pleasures of the body and neglect the treasures of the mind. Those are the things that last and those are the very ones that are neglected by the so-called teachers of this world, and we do not refer just to those in the classroom. Your politicians and those in government are the ones who are in many cases polluting the minds and bodies of the young.

And what sort of future generations are going to govern this planet of yours? Anarchy is what we can see, lawlessness and no respect for authority, and we can say in all honesty who can blame them, when the role models that are paraded before them have no real substance to them at all. Life today is like a glittering bauble, all show on the outside and nothing inside, just a hollow shell. In the distant past those who were thought of as the *Elders* were looked upon as those who knew what was right and proper in the living of their lives Where are your *elders* of today? We cannot see them! So-called *pop idols* are put up as examples to follow and what happens when the young and gullible do the following? We see *chaos* and even more *chaos*!. The life of the family is not considered important any more, everyone it seems must be able to *do their own thing* and where does that lead to? More chaos! What you are inventing today is obsolete tomorrow. There is no stability to your lives, can you not see the utter futility of it all?

And what, you may say, is the answer to all of this? It is believing in something beyond what man can see with his eye. And that is *God*! Turn back to Him. It's not too late! When *God* was lived in everyone's life, the world was a much kinder and loving place, people cared about each other, families *were* families. It mattered then, it still can if only people stopped trying to outdo each other and instead tried living with each other in harmony and understanding. You have absolutely no idea of what horror and terror awaits you if you do not *mend your ways*. You are already witnessing the awful power of Nature when she unleashes it. *You cannot stop her*. You will now have to live with the consequences of your own folly. Namely, the polluting of your atmosphere, the destroying of your forests, and the poisoning of the waters of your planet. The manipulating of the *genes* of not only yourselves but your animals and crops as well! You do not know what you are unleashing when you tamper with nature. She will always get the better of you, believe us. Live *with* her not *against* her! That way you can still live in harmony, but do not leave it until it is too late to rectify the damage you are causing! Others on other planets did just what you are doing and where did it get them? No more life, just dead planets waiting for the end to come.

Is that what you want to happen to this one? Or don't you even care any more? We look into the future and it looks bleak to us, if you do not stop this headlong rush into obscurity.

Take the warning seriously. The remedy is in your own hands, but it starts within your *minds*. *Think*. *Think*. And again we must say *Think*! We will help you all we can but it is *you* who have to make the first move!

We will leave it there. We bid you farewell and believe us, it is a sad Farewell that we say to you. Bring back God into your lives, it really is the only way to live what is called a *good life*. Think upon what we have said and change your attitudes for if you don't…

Well you know the consequences!

Chapter 40

August 5th 2003

The Soul

Have you, when passing a mirror or even a shop window caught a reflection that is looking back at you and in that split second you don't recognise the person in the reflection? You stop and look again, yes, you are still there and it is you looking back. Who on earth was that other one that you saw? He didn't even look like you, at least not how you see yourself! But then do you see what others see? To them you might appear quite different to how you see yourself. And then again you'd probably find that no two people if asked to describe you would not totally agree on how they see you. And if they are together when this description is being aired, one might say to the other "Oh no, I wouldn't say that, they're…"

And so the differences would be voiced. And if you were in a position to hear their discourse, you might well think that they are not even talking about *you*! For you do not quite recognise this person they are discussing. So then who was that person that you thought you saw in that mirror reflection? If he wasn't the *you* that you recognise as *you*, just who was he? Could he be one of the other *you* that you have been told make up who you really are? Now if you were to multiply that one by seven, you would be nearer the mark as to who *you* really are

Now that will make you sit up!

You've been told about your Spirit 'body', but these others? Well that takes a bit of getting used to or even believing! And where, you may ask, do these other you reside? They can't all take turns, as it were, being within you, or even hovering around waiting to be identified. And why should you need all these other entities in the first place?

Well, just try and think about it for a while. You know that your Soul remains on the Soul plane and cannot of itself leave that plane of existence. So being an adventurous kind of 'Soul' it is allowed to use some of its creative powers to, as it were, enrol what you would term a number of body-like entities that can do the work for Soul and report back what they find out about the various spheres below that of the Soul plane!

Now don't think that when we use the term 'bodies' that that is what they are. They are not bodies in the human sense and yet they can take on that likeness if it is required! For on the Higher known places bodies are like 'light forms' ,that is their, shall we say, normal form, the likeness of a human form can be materialised, if that is the correct interpretation, if they either wish to be known or *seen*. And usually they are only *seen* by their lower representative on the plane below, and so it goes on until they reach that one that you upon Earth call the 'Spirit Realm'.

Now sometimes one of the 'Higher ones' for reasons known only to themselves actually materialise upon the Earth plane. Not for very long because the vibrationary system that we all use has to be adjusted to suit the denser planet of Earth, and this does require quite an effort on the part of the visitor! So it could well be one of these Higher you that you may see from time to time! They are *all you* in varying degrees, and so do not all look alike and yet there is a similarity about them that enables you upon the Earth to know that the one you are seeing is *you*. They only use this resemblance form for *your benefit*, for reasons that are unknown to us your Earth likeness seems to remain as a reference form for quite a long time upon the various realms, but it lasts *only* as long as *you* wish it to, or require it to. One day you will present yourself to your Soul and you will be an amalgamation of all of your various *selves*, so you would probably be unrecognisable as your Earth bound physical entity!

And then what you wonder?
You will be assessed as it were by your Soul and then Soul will present itself to those of the Higher assembly, who will assess all that they are shown and incidentally all that they secretly know about each individual Soul!

When 'they' have come to a conclusion and when 'they' are all in agreement, then they summon Soul once more and then inform Soul if it is now ready to proceed to the Higher realms beyond the Soul plane. If it is not ready, then Soul is given careful instructions as to what is needed for it to be in a position to proceed with its fellow Soul travellers on the upward journey of fulfilment!

There is always 'movement' going on, so if soul has to remain for a period it does not lose out because of it, for there are always more fellow travellers to belong to. Souls never question the Higher ones, for they know that what is done is done for their own good, for eventually it is Soul's aim to be re-united with its creator, in whatever capacity the Creator decides! That would be the ultimate goal.

We are told we can go no further with this discourse and so reluctantly we will bid you all a Farewell and may the Blessings of those upon High be a comfort to you in your journey upon this plane of Earth.

Chapter 41

May 1st 2004

The Mortal Body

What is this mortal body that we try to take care of all through our Earthly existence?

It is but flesh and bone that one day we must vacate and leave it behind to return to the Earth from whence it came. To perhaps one day become unearthed to reveal just a few bones, a skeleton that when devoid of its fleshly covering is hardly identifiable as the human being it once was. And this is what we inhabit, it is what the Spirit has to call its home when it is trapped in the case of flesh and bone!

So what of this Spirit that boasts immortality? What is it really like? Many people think that their Spirit is a mirror image of their physical body and why on earth should we want that to be the case when the physical body is only a temporary covering, used for the purpose of being host to the real one that we are told is immortal? This physical garment is just a biological product of genes and tissue and in need of constant replenishment to keep it in an active state! Though even that cannot stop its deterioration which is inevitable and usually accompanied by illness and disease.

Looking at it in that light this human body is hardly the perfect specimen to house a Spirit counterpart. Yet, it must have its uses mustn't it?

So what are they if they are to be of value to the continued life of the Spirit that dwells within it?

What is it that we, when in this human body, have to learn that can be of use and value to our real self? For we are informed that the World of the Spirit is far, far superior to the Earthly one in every way. And what the Spirit can achieve upon that sphere would astonish us as human beings!

Yet when we look around us at our world, and see the beauty of it, even if we seem to be destroying it as fast as we can! The seasons, the morning sun and the night-time moons, the birds, the beasts, the trees, the flowers, in fact all the things that go to make up what we loosely call life. Those we call our family, our father, our mother, brothers and sisters, we can it would seem count ourselves very fortunate to be given this opportunity of experiencing life upon this dense planet we call Earth and home. And when we start to look at it from the right perspective we can see that this life is important to that other one that one day we return to. And you notice we say 'return to', which implies that we must have come from it in the first place, if we are to return to it! So this life upon the Earth plane must teach us what we need to learn about ourselves, that we were unaware of upon that other sphere of existence.

So assuming that when we leave this Earth to return to the world of the Spirit with this added knowledge, why do we have to keep coming back to the Earth plane? It is because within one life span we cannot hope to learn all that we need to know that will enable us to continue our interrupted life upon that other sphere. For we are told that this first plane of the Spirit world that we go to upon leaving this Earth one is but one of many more we will, in the course of our eventual return to our prime source of creation, have to reside upon in our upward journey back to the Godhead. Learning, loving ourselves, so that when we reach that state of perfection we will be worthy to be part of it. It seems such a roundabout way doesn't it to get back to where we started out from. And yet that is what *God* intended for us. We have to experience not only imperfection but hardship and heartache. That enables the Soul to realise that the gift of *Life* that *God* bestows upon us shows us *He* too knows these things, and as *He* has triumphed over them, then we can also, and be better for being allowed to understand that *Life* is for *living* and overcoming whatever it may throw at us. For we do have *God* on our side. He knows what we need and what is best for us. Our character is formed by what we experience and that is what we take with us on our journey through all of our lives and whatever sphere we are upon. *God* is always there pointing the way back to where one day we will be with Him in Paradise!

So that Earth journey was necessary wasn't it? It started us thinking and in thinking we began to understand and in the understanding we progressed. Life when viewed like that can be seen to have a purpose. A Divine purpose. Travel the path of righteousness for it leads all the way back to *God*.

And so we bid you Farewell little travellers upon the Earth. We have been where you are and so we can appreciate what you are going through – but know that where *we* are *now* you too will be one day. All the efforts are worth it. Believe that, for it is the Truth!

Farewell and may God's blessing be upon you now and in the coming days. Farewell.

Farewell, Brother Scribe, Farewell. God Bless You.

Chapter 42

March 13th 2003

Meditation

Meditation!

What can we say about that word? To each person Meditation means something that is personal to them and no one else, for in your Meditation you are seeking a communion with God. You are entering into the Holy of Holies to be in the presence of the Creator of all that there is and so you will no doubt feel what is it that I must do? What is expected of me? Do I pray? Do I sit quietly and wait? What else must I do?

Well dear friend, the first thing you must do is to cast aside all the thoughts of the day and yes, beyond, for thoughts tend to build up and stay at the back of your mind waiting for something to trigger them into action once again. You must learn how to quieten those thoughts and that is not easy. But do not strain, as it were, to push them aside. Try and relax. Do not think, do not even try to visualise anything in particular, just be still and gradually you will find that you become enveloped in an embracing stillness. You are part of the whole universe. There will be a form of darkness that seems to envelope your whole being, mind and body. But the darkness is not really dark for it is gently moving about, and you will begin to see that what appeared to be an empty space is in reality alive and part of you. Just remain still and quiet and know that no harm can come to you for you are protected by those whom you call your guides and helpers. Even though you may not be aware of their presence!

You are now sensing that there is something that wants to attract your attention, but that is only your brain trying to assert its authority. Ignore it. Just look ahead of you within yourself. Gradually you will become at peace again. Somewhere from within you, you will hear a faint murmur, like the gentle movement of water; a stream that is flowing through your whole body, starting at the crown of your head and gradually infusing your whole being until it reaches your very toes. There it will flow out, taking away all aches and pains and leaving you with a warm glow of sheer contentment.

Now it is time for you to have your visualisation, but it is not *you* who is doing the visualising, it is coming to you from afar. Just accept what it is, for it is for you and you alone, it doesn't matter if afterwards you cannot recall what it is that you have experienced but it has been of benefit to you. You have received the *love of God*, for He works in mysterious ways. No need to ask, for it is given freely and it is, when it is needed, that you not only receive it but you know that you have. Just remain quiet and gently become aware of who you are. You have received in your meditation what it is that you needed and not perhaps what it is that you thought you should have.

With each meditation you will find that 'losing yourself' will become easier and so you will slip into this reverie of the Spirit and become closer to the source of all creation and inspiration! Remember meditation is for *you* and *you* alone. Learn from each journey that you take and in time you will recognise the benefits that are being bestowed upon you, in your union with your God. Peace be with you dear friends, peace of mind and of body.

Remember you are the temple wherein God dwells. Make it a fit dwelling place for the almighty one.

Farewell, farewell, farewell.

Chapter 43

March 15th 2003

The Unknown Universe!

'The unknown'

And what is this unknown? Of course one could say 'the world of the Spirit', which to those upon the Earth plane is somewhat unknown.

To many people we must seem almost like an alien species that is written about in your books. Well, we can quite understand that, for after all most people will never have seen what we will term a 'physical Spirit', for that is what we are. Just as physical in appearance as you upon Earth! But of course that only goes for us who actually dwell upon the World called Spirit! Which incidentally is a 'Real World' and not some *airy fairy* place of existence conjured up in the mind of a magician.

Our world, which of course is *yours* as well, is in truth far more real, and yes solid, as yours that at present you dwell upon. But because it cannot be seen or touched by those upon Earth it remains something of an enigma. Does it really exist? How can it be proved? Where is this Spiritual world? All questions that do require answers and, yes, explanations.

To most people, Earth is not only their plane of existence it is the *only one* that they really know about. All other so-called

Worlds are purely hypothetical until actually proved by your members of the scientific criteria! You look up to the heavens and see millions of stars and galaxies, but they are only things in outer space, you have not yet proved to yourselves that they really do exist let alone have what you would term populations upon them!

You are at present unable to actually probe those areas of space that are the homelands of these other worlds. They have to remain what you think of as mysteries for a little while longer for those upon your planet. You are not *ready* to actually venture out let alone dwell upon those outer spheres of existence. And when we say *you are not ready* that is exactly what we mean. You are *not* ready either physically, mentally or spiritually to join with those who dwell upon those planets of the unknown. You seem to be trying to venture where you are not yet welcome, or for that matter would be accepted!

Think upon that. There are civilisations *out there* so far advanced that you could not possibly understand them. You would appear alongside of them as somewhat like a primitive savage race of almost an unknown species! You would be looked upon as quaint beings from an ancient world that they would be surprised are still in existence!

There are so many forms of life that exist that you have absolutely no comprehension of. You just could not, in your so-called wildest dreams, imagine their normal lifestyle. Their 'technology' is so far advanced as to be completely beyond your most advanced brains in your scientific fields of discovery.

We know of their existence and yes, we have been privileged to communicate with them and we are astounded at what we have seen. But we only observe them. We as yet do not dwell upon those planes of existence.

You see dear friends, 'they' are in a different time scale of evolvement in the so called spiral of evolution. We don't all progress at the same rate, or even in the same direction. Don't accept that at face value, for it does not convey what is really meant by 'same direction'. We leave it at that!

Life, in all its complexities, cannot as yet be explained in terms that could satisfy the human brain at present. So you must just accept that what we tell you is sufficient for you to comprehend now. In the future, yes, you will understand, but not for a very, very long time and then only when you have matured sufficiently to be accepted by those of higher intelligence and we do not mean to insult you, we just state a fact!

You peoples of the Earth have so much to re-learn about yourselves, you really have not begun to try to understand who and what you are and why you *are where you are*! The purpose is to enlighten not only your physical vehicle but also the one that dwells within. When you have accepted that fact, and here we are talking about the majority and not the thinking minority that at present are looked upon as somewhat of, what you term, as a 'cranky disposition', and all because most people are preoccupied with this physical existence and do not wish to delve into the world of the unknown in case it might make them sit up and alter their whole way of life and yet that is exactly what they must do if they are to become the beings that they were and are intended to be!

You look upon other species that your fiction writers have created for you as 'aliens' but it is *you* who are the 'aliens' not the other way around. Your writers portray those from outer space as people who wish to conquer you and subject you to all sorts of strange experiences. But think for a bit! What is it that your scientific people wish to do? They are the ones who wish to 'conquer' what they consider is their right to do.

And just what would they do *if* they did manage to 'conquer' an alien environment? You can't even live in harmony together upon Earth so how would you adapt to what would be an unknown planet of existence?!

No, dear friends. You just are *not* ready to be accepted by those other beings who dwell upon the spheres that you are seeking to discover with your very primitive forms of terrestrial transportation. Make your own world a safe dwelling place first before you explore outer space! Turn your minds to making this Earth a better habitation for *all peoples* and not just for the few.

You have got to learn how to live in harmony with one another and then perhaps you will be invited to *visit* those other continents that seem to beckon you in your imagination.

There is so much that you have to learn about and try to understand before you can really set out on these voyages of discovery. Be content to make this, *your* world, a fit place to live upon. Leave these other worlds alone. They will still be there long after this world of yours has become what to some would seem a forgotten planet and one just relegated to their history of the universe!

We seem to have dealt only with the physical side of your existence and not with the most important part to us, which is your *Spiritual counterpart.* Try to learn more about that aspect of your life's existence, for that is what you truly are: Spirit. That is the true aspect of who you are, bring that into line with your physical body and then you will see how things will fall into place, as it were.

Your journey then can begin. Fit yourselves mentally so that you are prepared when you are *contacted* by those who wish to be of help to you in your searching for the reasons for what is termed *life* and why it is that we are allowed to live it in the first place!

Such a lot for you to try and understand, so start with yourselves for that is a good starting point at least you are able to do that yourselves. You do not need to travel to outer space for that project, do you?

Your world is *yours* and *theirs* is *theirs.* Understand that and be patient in your desire for expansion.

Now we are told to end this night's discourse and so we will bid you farewell till next we meet again in Thought form!

Little scribe, farewell, and thank you.

Chapter 44

March 17th 2003

The Book of Life

S o often through life we stop and think to ourselves: where am I going? Where have I been? What has bought me to this stage in my life's cycle?

If we really stop and think it will be like turning the pages of a well read book, one that has been a familiar friend over the years. Each page that you can recall gives you a feeling of either pleasure or, sometimes, sadness. The page is written by your own hand, each one a signpost to the next one, and then when we come to the end of a chapter, we begin another, on a fresh page, with a fresh heading. As the book takes on a familiar shape you begin to see where the story of life is leading you. And so you begin to understand the reason why things have happened to you that have brought you to this part of your life.

Look back to the beginning, do you recognise the person on the pages as yourself or is it someone else? Familiar yes, but was that really you who did those things? You were young then, inexperienced and starting out on this career that we call life! Did you understand in those days of your youth what life was beginning to show you? Or were you so busy living it, that suddenly you were aware that oh so many chapters had been written and here you were in middle age, wondering where had all those years gone to.

Look back again. Read over those earlier chapters. Do you see a thread that has run through them? Are you now seeing the you that you are? And who are you? Are you this person who springs to life from those pages? Can you see where those early years have brought you to? Look hard before you turn over the pages, can you see the character that you have acquired, that is the now you? No, don't close the book. There are many more chapters for you to read. Where have you got to? Middle age? No, we've passed that stage now, what do those later chapters tell you?

Have you fulfilled all those earlier ambitions?

No, not all of them, but then circumstances perhaps were not always on your side and so you had to compromise, but perhaps they weren't all that important were they? You are now three quarters of the way through your book of life, pause again, turn back those pages again, what do you see? You have changed, haven't you? The person now on those pages has matured into a thinking being. What happened that made you take that turning in your life? Now you can see the reasoning behind that decision that you made, and it was the right one, wasn't it? No regrets. You were on the right path. Those that you met at that time, they did have an influence on your life, didn't they? And look, on that page you can see how you also influenced them, do you see the pattern that is emerging? Those next pages show how you started to think about where your life had brought you to, you had started to question and to wonder: was there more to this life than what you thought?

Yes, there must be. A few more pages on you can see you've started to think more deeply about what comes after this life has finished. Now you can see that what has come before has brought you to this stage in your book of life. The pages now reveal that you have begun searching for meanings. Meanings of what life is all about, and what it is for.

You have found out that there is more to you than you thought. There are others that seem to invade your thoughts. Are they part of you? Do they exist outside of your imagination? What effect do they have upon you, or more to the point, what effect have they *had* upon you, are they the ones that have set you thinking?

This next chapter reveals that those thoughts were positive ones, you had begun to understand that you are far more complex than that youthful person you once were. This chapter shows that you have started to understand why it is that you started out on this journey in the first place. Have you met some of those other 'you' that you wrote about in that last chapter?

Next page: yes, you have.

I see you thought it was in your dream state and that you didn't think the one you saw was really you, but it turned out that he was. Now that surprised you didn't it? And you were shown that there are more of you, but you were told that they would be revealed to you at a later date. Those next pages show that you had come to terms with not only yourself but this other side of life that had been hidden from you for so long.

These later pages are showing how far you have come in your understanding. They reveal a deeper meaning to your physical life. You now see just where you are and what it is that has brought you to this understanding.

We are nearly up to this last chapter, but there are many blank pages in this book yet to be written. I wonder what they will eventually reveal? Will this book of yours be worth reading? Will you look back upon those early pages and say: was that really me? Was I really like that? Did I really think like that? And yet you now know that yes, you were like that and yes, you did think like that and that is what has brought you to this enlightened part of your life.

It has all been truly worthwhile. All the heartaches, and sometimes the setbacks have all had their meaning. You now are who you are, and are ready to go forward knowing that what awaits you will be another book of life full of blank pages waiting for you to write upon. I wonder what that book will reveal when you review it prior to your next stage. Will some of the characters that you wrote about in that first volume be in your second one? Will you renew old acquaintances and friendships? Will you find yourself in their books of life? Wonder what they thought of you?

Life really is exciting isn't it? So much to cram into the few years that we spend upon this Earth. So make the most of it while you can. I look forward to reading your book of life someday. Perhaps you'll be reading mine as well! I suppose we had better leave this here for there is lots more for you to write about before you come to the last page and write the word 'finish'.

We bid you farewell dear friend. Don't forget, look back upon those pages, they make interesting reading!

Farewell little scribe, have you learnt anything from this night's discourse? Yes, we think you have.

Farewell till next time.

Chapter 45

March 20th 2003

Out There!

Welcome dear Brother on this fine morning. We are here to talk to you, via your pen, about thoughts that you recently had regarding other planets and their inhabitants.

I'm afraid you were wrong in your thoughts that maybe your other, Higher, self may be amongst those inhabitants. No, dear friend. Those other planets have their own form of populations. They are 'physical' if you like to use that term. They are not Spirit entities as you know them. Spirit counterparts of your known Earth remain in the Evolutionary spiral pertaining to that world! And so your so-called 'Higher Selves' would be on the sphere allotted to those inhabitants.

That is not to say that so called Spirit forms from our spiral of existence cannot visit those other planets, but only for the purpose of gaining knowledge or, if we are required, to offer assistance that we are proficient in.

Each planet or world has its own form of evolution just like yours. They have their Spirit counterparts as you have, but they are *separate* in the evolutionary scale. For some of them are very far advanced and so you could not possibly integrate with them on a one-to-one basis.

Do you follow what we are saying? Your world is for your form of 'human species' and theirs is for them. The two do *not* merge! This may come about in the far off distant future according to your time scale, but that is only speculation on our part. As you are aware 'time' as you perceive it is *not* the same for all dimensions. And travelling, as it were, from one time zone to another is not as yet possible for you people of the Earth!

There is much for you to learn about regarding 'time' before you can venture out of your time warp. So you will have to be patient and keep to your own sphere for the 'time being'!

Worlds, or planets, or spheres, whatever you wish to call them, are all at different levels of vibrations and evolvement. Some are very similar. Those that are in the same location, as it were, you would call 'neighbours', but in actual fact they maybe millions of so-called miles, or light years apart!

The universe that you inhabit is vast, vast, vast and is still expanding and so the time scales that you talk about are forever changing! Even yours may be 'speeded up' and your whole outlook regarding time will be different! You at present can not comprehend just what that would entail for your whole 'life cycle' would be changed.

We cannot explain to you just how that would affect your growth, for instance, and that would involve just one of the many changes that would be needed. Your whole mental outlook would alter, for 'time' to you then would be almost a 'thing of the past'!

That is as far as we are allowed to go at present in our explanations! Just accept that you are part of your 'worlds' transformation, and what transpires on it is only for you and no others. You are not yet ready to become an active participant in the universal Brotherhood. You stand, as it were, outside looking in. When you have, and here we are not being unkind, when you have 'grown up' then you will be instructed as to how your future lives are to be led for you to qualify for the amalgamation of your world with those others in the galaxy!

We observe the way your scientific bodies are trying to work out the means to travel and, shall we say, colonise those areas of space that they can perceive, but believe us they do not understand a fraction of what lies out there in your universe.

They experiment upon Earth with what they imagine is 'out there' waiting for them to explore, but how do they know that what they perceive is still out there and is a viable form of life force for them to dwell upon? 'Out there' life is forever changing, becoming, and then altering and either remaining an inert piece of formless matter, or maybe becoming a living and vibrating sphere of existence. Not known and not observed by those upon the planet Earth!

You may even find one day that there are many more living spheres floating around and yes, even disappearing when you have noted them, to begin orbiting in a completely different area of the known universe. You cannot take for granted what it is that you think you observe. Even your most advanced form of telescopic lenses cannot penetrate the gloom that exists in the far distant atmosphere! And even that word 'gloom' does not denote the actuality of what we have said! For gloom to you can just be the one sided visualisation of what is really existing in another dimension!

We started with the reason for your Spirit forms not actually living upon those other planets and so we return to that subject.

Each 'world' has its own spiritual counterpart. Its Blueprint, as it were, for its existence and each counterpart does *not integrate* with another. Each has its separate form of evolutionary progress, we do not all evolve at the same pace. That would never do. There would be a form of chaos to put it mildly! So be assured dear friend, your so-called 'Higher Selves' will live and evolve in the right area that has been designated to your Earth plane.

One day, when you reach these Higher realms, you will know more, and then you will be able to fulfil your destiny, so let that be sufficient for you at present. You have enough to satisfy your curiosity for now. Accept what we have tried to impart to you as facets of the one *truth*. Remember though that truth has many sides to it so use your intellect to interpret what we have said.

Farewell little scribe, farewell. Much for you to think about!

Chapter 46

March 21st 2003

Character, What is it?

Dear Brother, once again we bid you welcome.

You were restless and wondered why? Well it is we, your Brothers in Christ, who wish to converse with you. We wish to enlighten you regarding not only Spirit but also the physical body that you inhabit. So often when one starts to think about things, we turn our thoughts to not only this world but also the one that is called Spirit. We know that in some way they are joined, but the reason for this union sometimes seems to evade us.

How can this physical body be of use to us who are primarily Spirit? What can that body tell the other one what it already knows? And how can the mere fact of having lived upon the material planet called Earth fit us for the journey that awaits us in that Higher World?

Well, the physical body is merely the vehicle that we are allowed to use while upon the lower sphere, but it is not the body that is important, it is what it houses! Namely the *mind controller* of that body, for that is the essence of the Divinity that is the guiding force. And what is it that it is guiding? Or, shall we say, motivating? It is building up the character of the person that is called 'self', and where and what *is* this character and what is so important about it that it has to be nourished and given encouragement? That is the part that, together with the mind substance, travels upward on the Spiritual path when the body of the physical person is left behind.

But where and what is this 'character' that we speak of? Can you see it? Can you parade it in front of you and say 'this is my character'. What do you think of it? It is illusive, for though it forms your whole being it cannot be seen by the naked eye and yet it is observed by others, for character is the *you* that is visible, it is the basic structure that carries you through life. It is how you treat other people, it is how you confront your difficulties. In fact, it is the *basic you*. It is what you have acquired in your day to day living. No, it doesn't just happen or appear, it grows as you yourself grow. It gradually takes over your whole being and it is that part of you that is the visible portion of the God essence!

Character is what makes you. You are not born with it, it grows within you as you come into, shall we say, 'conflict with life'. For life is a form of battleground. Always decisions to be made of rights and wrongs and yes, in between. Everything in life is not black and white, there are many grey areas that go to make it up. But it is how you learn to cope with what life throws at you, that is what builds this elusive thing called character! It is how you mature into a thinking, caring human being. How often do you hear the comment 'Oh he has strength of character, that's what's pulled him through'?

And yet where is this thing called character? You can't put your finger on it and yet it is there staring you in the face all the time. We could say it is your Spirit side of your nature shining through, but to many people they would not quite understand that statement, and yet it is the Truth!

A person with what we will say is a 'good character', and that encompasses a great deal, is one who has either known, or even not known, or been aware that they have let their *Spirit side* govern their actions. So you see this journey upon the Earth plane has been worthwhile, for it has opened up that side of you that perhaps you were not even aware of!

So is this character that we speak of really our Spirit-self making itself felt in our daily lives? You will argue that we are all Spirits, so what has that to do with this thing called character? Well the formation of character is the allowing of the Spirit essence to flow through our every action in our daily lives. It allows us to be a decent human being, one who cares about others and how life is affecting them, especially when it seems to have dealt them a bad hand. But if they have allowed their Spirit counterpart to help them in their life, they will be able to overcome those difficulties that perhaps to another person would seem insurmountable. You see this is where character comes into its own. It is the ability to stand firm in the face of adversity and try to overcome those difficulties of life that are, in reality, part of this character building that we speak of. It's acknowledging that aspect of us that we call our Spirit, that is what God has endowed us with, that carries us through all these trials and tribulations, yes, and also all the good times that compensate us for them.

This character that we have dwelt upon is what we have come to Earth to promote and so take with us on our upward journey. For character is the human side of our Spiritual nature. It has opened up for the Spiritual side the knowledge that it possesses yet perhaps is not aware of until it has been tempered by the stay upon the Earth with all its problems and vicissitudes that accompany us through our lifetime upon Earth. It is this training ground that we need to release what is within our Spirit that lies dormant until awakened by the physical vehicle we call our body! This Spirit shines through those who have allowed their character to be formed by it. People do notice it, even if they cannot quite put their finger on it. They sense what it is that they cannot quite understand. So they say 'hasn't so and so a lovely character?' What they really mean is 'hasn't so and so a lovely Spirit'!

What's in a name? It doesn't really matter what it is called as long as it is there for all to see and by seeing it feeling the better for it. So accept that the building of your character is the allowing your Spirit to govern your life, your actions, your thoughts; in fact becoming a good character in every sense of the word.

That is what life upon Earth is all about. The building of your character, which is the liberating of your Spirit in the knowledge of who it is, and why it is and what it is! It is the aspect of the Divinity in action.

We leave you with our blessings and may peace be with you now and always.

Chapter 47

March 23rd 2003

The Word "Spirit"!

So often when two or more people are gathered together and the word 'Spirit' comes up you can almost feel the change in the atmosphere!

Here we are talking about conversations that occur at, shall we say, social gatherings. People are immediately interested in what perhaps one person is talking about. They want to know more and yet somehow they are a little apprehensive, for they are not sure if what they are going to hear will effect them. Some will listen out of curiosity, others maybe genuine seekers, then there are others who want to scoff at what they are being told. Altogether the air becomes charged, each person wondering what it is that they are going to hear and will they feel any different after hearing it!

So often, people who are interested in learning about the World of the Spirit are looked upon by the majority as being somewhat like 'cranks'. As if believing in the 'after life', a very peculiar expression we feel, makes them somewhat peculiar to the rest of society: as if they have some sort of unknown powers and so people are curious as to what is being told them. They, in a way, hope for something strange to happen and yet feel a little bit apprehensive in case if it does it will do 'something' to them! Yet the people who do posses this esoteric knowledge are no different to the rest of the population. They eat, sleep and drink, just the same as others, but they are the *thinkers* of this world of yours. They want to know what it is that awaits them when they transcend to the next sphere of learning.

To many people the word 'Spirit' makes them think of séances, table rapping and all sorts of exotic goings on. When Spirit, that is the other side of you the physical vehicle, is just an extension of that seen body. The only difference being that it is the permanent one, not like the physical body which will one day return to dust, part of the universe from which it comes from!

Spirit, and here we talk not only of the person but the world to which it belongs, should not be this weird body or substance that many people think of. It is the real you. Once upon a time long, long ago, man and Spirit were united as one! They walked and talked together, not as strangers but as brothers. There are still people upon this planet of yours that are still in that form of communication. Look at the Aborigines of Australia. They haven't quite lost this act of communion, but sadly they are losing this ability because of their desire to become what others term 'civilised'! But in so doing, that God given gift is being diluted.

Such a sad thing to behold. If only people would realise that their own Spirit counterpart is closer to them than they know. There were civilisations that no longer exist that had this knowledge, but they too lost it through abuse of this gift.

If only it could be resurrected once more and *used* in its proper manner and that is to lead a good and true life as God intended it to be! Spirit was never meant to be separate from man's physical body. It was his companion, the part of him that was in union with the Almighty. That is why in your Holy book, and others you hear of, this communion with God was a fact and not a fantasy. Man was originally the manifested part of the Almighty himself. A son of God in actuality, and when he lived by the principles that God had given him you had what you have read as the *Golden Age*.

God was not a far off creature but was part of the everyday existence of Earth man. Now He has been relegated to somewhere beyond the Heavens, sitting in perpetual judgement of those upon Earth. He does nothing of the kind. *You* are the *judges* of your own actions, you are responsible and no one else. Don't cry to God when things go wrong, and hope somehow that he will put them right until the next time that *you* instigate, what you call, circumstances that are beyond you! If you really stop to think you will know that adverse circumstances are usually brought about by Man himself, because of his greed and his selfishness towards his fellow man and, yes, to those other creatures of Gods creation! We cannot in out present state hope to walk and talk once more with God the Father, we have become too preoccupied with our own so-called importance. But we *need God* more than *He needs us.* Bring Him back into your daily lives. Don't wait until you have left this Earth and are with us in Spirit, where we know God as a reality and not the illusive being that you think of Him as.

Those of you who are gifted with the wisdom and knowledge of what you call the *World beyond,* and those who dwell there, when you speak of those things to those who may enquire of you, tell them of the normality of that World. Let them understand that it is not to be feared or thought of as a place of strangeness and full of weird goings on! It is a normal habitat where normal people live. Where they will one day return to, to resume their interrupted life upon that realm. Clear away their misconceptions of that World. Let them know that *they* are Spirit as well as physical body and that there's nothing strange or peculiar about it! They've got to find out one day and the sooner they do, the better their lives will become.

In fact, this world will be a better place when that knowledge is accepted universally. Show people that those who have this knowledge already are just ordinary human beings, nothing strange about them, no hidden tricks up their sleeves to deceive the unwary. All these strange sects that have sprung up only confuse people, especially the gullible ones who quite often are genuinely searching for answers to their inner questions. Let them see there is nothing wrong in wanting to know the *Why of Life* but let them see that the answer is simple. Talk to God, bring Him into your daily life. *Don't shut Him* out, for in reality He dwells within you. He is the part of you that knows what is right and what is wrong. He is the Spirit within. Let Him, that is *you*, live the life that you know you should be living and when you do that you will have found *God*, you don't have to wait until some future date, when to find Him may be too late for you to do anything about it!

Chapter 48

April 2nd 2003

To Dream!

D o not worry dear friend, this talk is from us and is not part of your imaginative process. We shall begin with the words 'What is belief?'

Belief is an understanding of what has not only been told to you but is what you feel inside. A feeling that all is not as it may appear to be when viewed not only with the physical eye but with the brain as well. So much that has been given to you has to be taken, as it were, on trust. Either you accept that or you reject it. But if you reject it, what are you left with? Uncertainty, for part of you longs to know that what you have been told, or even read, is the truth.

But so much just cannot be verified to your own physical satisfaction. So you are somewhat in a dilemma, do you go along with that has been said and read or do you query it? But even then just to query something that you cannot verify for yourself does not mean that it is not true. That is where your own intuition takes over, you feel, yes, that does sound like the truth and you hope and pray that it is. We do our best to help you to find the truth that is within you. A truth that you know for yourself, because you not only want to believe it but because you know that the alternative would be a blank canvas, and so you would be left, as it were, with nothing to, shall we say, cling on to!

Life itself is a form of not knowing, day by day you begin to piece together what it is that life is showing you. You have something positive and tangible to grapple with, and so you can say to yourself, this is the truth because I am living it. But what about that other life that is only known by your inner self, that you sometimes wonder if it is real or just a wishful thought, one that you hope is a reality and not from your imagination.

You know from personal experience that often in your dream state you know that you have been somewhere not in this physical world, but nevertheless still a world of reality. Though not always are you able to recollect all the scenes that you have lived through in your so-called dream. So often these *true dreams* really are *true* and not figments of your brain conjured up to either give you enjoyment or pleasure, though we must admit that some dreams can be just the opposite. But, if thought, about there is usually a rational explanation, either a late supper, or even something that has happened to you during the daylight hours, and these forms of dreaming can be dismissed for they have not conveyed to you truth but, rather, fiction!

Whereas those dreams that somehow you can remember positive fragments of are the true reality of where you have been living while out of your physical body. You have been where we shall say is a dream world of reality. A place of true existence, one that has been teaching you something that you needed to know. But then you will say: 'Why can't I remember it *all* and not just fragments, what good are they to me?' Well dear friend, those *dreams* are not for your physical body but for the so-called Spiritual one. That one needs *learning experiences* just the same as your physical body does. And if you did but know it, those sojourning upon that other realm really do have their repercussions on your physical existence. Have you not wondered sometimes and thought 'I've done this before' and yet you know that you haven't in your physical body so where did you do this thing if not in the physical?

The answer is: in your dream world. The real world that you co-exist with, even if you are not always aware of its true existence. That is why when you are told or perhaps read in a book certain things, you *know*, you really do, that it is the *truth*. Its not just wishful thinking. Your other life is making itself known to you, do not push it aside, learn from it! You may not always be aware of the lessons you have learnt while in your dream world, but they do have a bearing upon your physical life. You often cope with situations because you have already done so in your *dream state* and so the situation is not only familiar, but it is as if it were known about beforehand and has been overcome.

So you see those dream encounters were of positive use, you learnt a lesson before actually having to experience it physically! There is so much more to our lives than just this earthly one that we have to live. We are a complex piece of workmanship, there are many facets to our personality that we call 'me'. There are those other 'me' that also have their own existence but who are, nevertheless, still 'me'. Sometimes, very rarely, they all come together, as it were, like a sheath one upon another, interpenetrating each other until the whole vibrationary force fills you. And then you *know*, yes, you *know*, and the truth is revealed to you, so that when someone perhaps queries what you have said you reply: 'But I know, I just do!' You may not remember how you know, but inwardly you know that it is so! So do not be daunted or put off if someone says to you 'Well can you prove it?'. You don't have to prove it to them for you know it is true for yourself. They must wait until they too have experienced this inner knowledge for themselves! Truth, or shall we say the knowing of it, comes from within. That is the Spiritual truth that should be your guiding force. You can only say what you yourself know and feel, it is up to the enquirer to make of it what they will.

Everyone does not see the truth in the same way. To some it may never be revealed, while to others it comes naturally and why?

Because they have learned it by experiencing it for themselves, and that can never be taken away from them. Each person lives their many lives in their own way. Those who think and are searching reach the truth more easily than those who only pick at it but who in their hearts do not, or shall we say, *are* not yet ready to accept what it is they are being shown!

Just go on as you are, give out what you know and feel is what to you is the truth and leave it at that! It is by example that others will begin to know that there is more to life than just this physical existence, however important it is while it is being lived, and of course it is important but it is not the only one of importance, is it?

We think we will leave this discussion on that point. Go on searching dear friends, you are on the right path. The inner knowledge is what sustains you in your outward existence, so make good use of it, and remember, not all *dreams* are *dreams* as you think you know them. Some *dreams* are what you are living now in your physical body. Sleep is not always necessary for what you may term a dream state! Something for you to think upon is it not?

Chapter 49

April 3rd 2003

Why?

A s you travel on your pathway through life you often stop and think, where have I come from and, yes, I think I know where I'm going to but what does it all mean?

To some, this Earth life seems so hard and uncompromising that it is no wonder that the thoughts that cross their minds are ones of scepticism as to the 'why' of it all. And yet again to others they find that this life offers them so much that to question it never occurs to them. So why is it that one seems to be favoured and another not?

That question has vexed people all through the ages and will no doubt continue to do so as long as people live upon this Earth and yet this plane is only a temporary one in our journey through life. Or rather our journey through the many lives that not only await us but that we have already lived!

When you view your sojourn upon this Earth and think about why it is that you find yourself here, you should stop and say to yourself, if this is one of many, well where have they taken me to. If I have to remain on this plane of existence for three score years and ten, what have those other lives taught me.

Or perhaps they haven't! For this life we are told is a training ground. One that is to fit us for the next step on the upward path back to where we originally came from! Looking at it like that it is no wonder that you feel perplexed and think has it all been worth it, especially if you are one of the unfortunate ones whose life upon this Earth is one of toil and trouble!

But what has brought you to this conclusion? Could it be that your lessons have not been learnt? And where were these so called lessons being taught you? Here on Earth? Or elsewhere? And if elsewhere, why don't we know of them?! Puzzles, puzzles, and I'm afraid they will have to remain so until we can begin to see where it is that we now stand in relation to what is termed 'eternity' to most people. At least those in the Western Hemisphere. This life that they are living is the only one that concerns them, they fondly think that when it is time for them to shed this fleshly garment, that Heaven awaits them, a sort of reward for having had to be here on Earth in the first place!

But that is because they do not really think coherently, and religion as such is not much help in answering their questions as to why they are here in the first place.
But 'first place' is the wrong expression, for this 'place' is definitely *not* the first one! It is, shall we say, one of the many that we have to experience on our upward journeying! We *all* start out, as it were, from a far distant form of existence, one that we cannot even remember and yet there is always a nagging feeling that perhaps we don't really belong here and that our real home must be somewhere else. That is if you are one of the thinking class of humanity! And if you are then your eyes have been opened and you really are on your upward journey. This life then can be seen for what it is, a stepping stone, but to some a millstone that seems to hold them back from what they feel is their real self.

We have all gone through this form of self analysis, and if we are sensible then we can see the logic of it all. But it would seem it takes us many lives before we come to that conclusion. If only there was a short cut, we feel, but unfortunately there is not. Life is a long time of living and we should be grateful for that really, if we are to eventually be worthy to become co-workers with our Creator. For that is the ultimate goal of all souls if they did but know it!

Now you will think 'how can this life upon this Earth fit us for that privilege?'. Well think dear friend, and you will know then why it is that we have to travel this particular path so many times before we are fit to proceed to the next plane of existence permanently. By which we mean, no more need to come back to this Earth to learn the lessons of life upon it!

If you look around at your fellow travellers and yes, your Nations that are made up of them you will understand why it is that it takes so long to reach what you could term a civilised form of existence. Upon this Earth we see ourselves not as we really are but as we imagine we are, and how often can you really feel content with what you see?! Not many of us can say with hand on heart, 'I do like what I see' and really mean it.

We are but mortal while upon this sphere. Immortality may await us but we are not yet ready to put on that garb. Try and learn what it is that we are here for, and then make the effort to make it a better life, not only for yourself but for others as well. For who knows you may be neighbours for many lifetimes in this upward spiral of ours! Think earnestly about the 'life to come', for that is the real one. Start to prepare now, don't wait until it is time for you to leave this one. If you live this one as best you can and with the inner knowledge that you, as thinkers, know about then your sojourns upon this Earth can become a thing of the past for you. And then you can really begin to *live* in the realm of the so-called 'Spirit'. Not journeys *end* but journeys *beginning*. Look forward to renewing your life there for that is where you have come from in your lives of expectation!

There are many more for you to experience and many more for

you to live upon and begin to understand the meaning for them. Death of the body is the release that enables you to start afresh. Lessons learnt, you are now ready to take your rightful place where you belong. Earth is but a resting place before the real life that you belong to can start once more. What you have learnt there will help you in your discovery of who you are and where you are in the scheme of things! Nothing lost, nothing wasted, all put to good use, all part of this thing we call 'life'.

Chapter 50

April 12th 2003

The Flower of Truth

'Solomon in all His glory was not arrayed like one of these.'

Words from your scriptures and what was it that is said of as 'one of these'? It was the Lilies of the field! A simple beautiful flower that in those days grew in profusion, wild and free.

Do you understand the underlying reason for that statement? It is the simple things of the Earth that are a pleasure to God. Not all of the gorgeous trappings and cloths of gold that adorn not only a person, but also the edifice that houses him!

God sees beneath all the splendour and what does He behold? The outward shows conceals something that if seen by mortal eyes would make you avert your gaze! The word *church* has been much misrepresented over the centuries. It has become not a true place of worship but one where neighbours vie with each other as to who should be seen either in their so-called finery or their position in the building! *No one is first in God's house* and *no one* is *last*!!

A footstool on a mountain top is where God is to be found. And that dear friend, does not mean what you think! 'A mountain top' is in the heart of the true worshipper of God. Free and open, not mumbling words that now have lost their meaning to most people.

Talk to God in simple language and not in repetitive phrases and platitudes, always asking and never giving!

God is not a God of the Old Testament. *He Never Was*! That was Man's invention and used to keep under subjection wayward people, putting fear into their hearts instead of *love*. He is all that that word implies and more. You cannot conceive of the true nature of *God* for your idea of love is a rather feeble one when put alongside that of the Almighty. Love in its true sense is humble, gentle, kind, self effacing, and above all *true*! To really *love* is to become the person to whom you are showing it to. Being completely unselfish and doing to another what you in turn would wish to be done to you.

That is the bounty of God's love for all of his fellow creatures, be they large or small, seen or unseen. Nothing can exist without the love of God breathing into it His very own *life force*. Be like the lilies of the field, pure and simple, and may the beauty of that flower be the Spirit within you, and shine forth all around you as well as within.

Be simple in all that you do and think. Treasure the new born child, for that child may grow up to be a Saviour of Mankind! Of whatever race or colour we all come from the one Father and so we are brothers under the skin. We are one family. Learn to live as one and that does not mean that you always have to agree with each other. Learn to live and let live. Agree to differ, but let it not arouse anger within your heart, there is room for everyone upon this beautiful Earth of yours. God created a perfect paradise for you to live in and learn from. Perfection has to be worked at before it attains that virtue and that is what Man has been given this life, to learn how he can become what he was originally, when in the bosom of the Father. Perfection, another word for *love* in all its varied aspects! It can be achieved if you only become the unselfish person that God originally created. You are part of Him as He is in fact the visible part of Himself in you!

No need to be a Solomon, even with all of his wisdom, he could not compete with the flowers of the field in their simplicity. Be like them, show God that you do understand what He has told you. Christ was born in a manger, a simple place, not a palace, and yet he rose to become a King. King of all that there is. A King for everyone, whoever they happen to be. So when you use His name when in supplication to God, use it with reverence, for Christ also dwells within you and to take that name in vain is doing yourself *no service* believe me.

Peace be with you.

Chapter 51

April 13th 2003

In the Beginning!

We take you on a journey little Brother, back, back, back to the beginning; no, not of time but of *your beginning*. We will speak, as it were, about another being, or *beings,* but you are to accept if you wish that it applies to you as to others.

We begin with you as an 'embryo', a thought form of the Divine Creator. You resemble, as it were, a minute tadpole-like creature swimming around in a milky like substance, quite content. You are in this state for quite a long time, until is has been decided that it is your turn and time for you to emerge from this stage and become a 'light force' of thought substance. You are then placed in a vapour like substance where you will remain in a sleep state.

When it has been deemed that you are ready, you are gently awakened from your sleep state and you emerge as a completed light form with a thinking organ that is *the real* you. You then merge with other light forms in a school-like existence and here you are to be taught about what the lives ahead of you are for. You are shown in thought form various picture-like creations, that is creations of the humanities! You are given time to think about these forms and if you wish to use one for yourself, male or female, though to you at this stage you are not aware of the difference. Once you have decided upon the picture of your choice, you are taken to an area that is put aside for the sole purpose of showing you how by thought you can become that body form. When you have adjusted to this phenomena, you are then shown how to animate this being that is to become your very own life being on all spheres.

Now you and your protégé are placed together and a form of sleep invades your body. When *you,* the original light body of mind substance, awakes you now have a body that is yours to animate and live within. More adjusting and then you are ready for the next stage in your *evolution downwards* to the spheres and planes below. The ones that you upon Earth call the *Spirit.*

In your present state you would not be able to exist upon those lower spheres and so you must put on a cloak of protection! In other words a denser body type organ. You are shown how to do this, and corrected if necessary. You now posses not one but *three* life forms, but still you will need more before reaching your ultimate goal called 'Earth'. The first one has remained where it originated and the second now does the same, this one has an identity of its own and can live upon that sphere on which it was created, though it is linked by thought waves to the third and subsequent bodies of existence.

This procedure is repeated until you are in the sphere adjoining the Earth one. You now resemble a solid mobile dense Earth body, though you are still Spirit but soon to be capable of living upon that planet. Now how do you get to that one? Not as a fully-grown adult, I'm afraid! You are shown like a cinematograph film, various lives that you can live from cradle to the grave. Once you have decided upon the one that seems to appeal to you, you are then shown various 'parent type' pictures and it is up to you to decide upon this. You are not influenced in any way, it is entirely up to you, and if you make a mistake then you must learn to live with it, for that is the whole purpose of your journey to Earth, to learn and know who and what you are!.

Now that you have decided upon the parent or parents that you wish to start your life with you are allowed to, as it were, rest and sleep. When you awake you are being born and the body that remains is now what is known as 'your Spirit', your guiding force for the infant that you have now become!

So starts your round of life cycles from one incarnation to the next. Each one teaching you the true meanings of life, and that covers all its aspects, good and bad and in-between!

You learn, and your 'spirit' is also learning and this information is not lost for it is transmitted from one to the other ever upward to the embryo that we call our Soul. Your incarnations upon Earth will be varied and take in many, many centuries of Earth time. You will encounter quite often the same people who have made your life what it is: parents, relatives, friends, partners, and yes, even what you may term enemies, though that need not be of the warring kind!

Your lives will take on a pattern, if you choose to learn from them and take heed of what they are teaching you. Once you have reached the stage where you yourself know what you have learnt all that you feel you need to know from the Earth life then you are ready to resume your journey back to where you originally came from!

But! There are many more lives for you to live before that can transpire.

Your next World, which is the one you call Spirit, is finer, more fluid and vibrates at a higher rate. You are now upon the world of 'thought building' and 'thought illusion'. You are to be taught how to use thought constructively, to differentiate between what is real and what may seem to be real! In other words, illusion. Illusion of reality and the knowledge that not all of reality is real!

You are part of where you are. You feel and know about what it is that you observe including other people, if you get their permission to do so! The life on this realm is to prepare you for the one to come, all stepping stones on the pathway back home!

We feel that that is where we will bid you farewell. There is so much for you to learn about in the art of living, and one step at a time is the best way of doing it, even if you would like more on the subject, you must be patient.

You have in the past been given insights into the life that awaits you once you leave this earthly body for good. So accept that we can only give what we are allowed to, at any given time.

Chapter 52

April 15th 2003

The Tool Called "Thought"

So often as persons approach, shall we say, old age, they begin to wonder not only what their life has been all about but more to the point where will this next one lead them to. That is if they think upon those lives. Sadly, many people think that the earthly life is the one and only, and there again others look forward to what they imagine is the Heaven that awaits them!

Difficult to try and convince the sceptics and those whose fantasy they hope will become reality.

But this next world, or stage, in the evolution process is not at all like what most people think. You have left behind the outworn mortal shell and you return to your Spiritual body of light. This is your now permanent body of existence. Your spirit body was always there and so is in harmony with the world of the Spirit. You will then rationalise that as Spirit you should be quite 'at home' so why all the fuss about being reunited with it?

Well dear friend, you have spent a lifetime upon the Earth plane and have acquired a lot of unnecessary baggage. That is *thought* baggage! This has to be sifted through and what is not relevant to your present whereabouts, discarded. No dear friend, it has not been wasted. It served its purpose and has helped to make of you what you now are. But remember, you still have your own thoughts and here they will grow and sustain you through these realms of exploration!

We are speaking of when it is your time to leave the Earth sphere for good. If you are, shall we say, 'in transit' then your life here is somewhat different. It may appear to you as almost like a holiday, for everything is so exciting. But for you who are to return to Earth it is not your permanent existence, unlike those whose home it now is! Those who are as we have said 'in transit' do mix with those permanent residents for they are still at the learning stage and need help and advice and if they follow what is shown to them then they benefit extremely and when next they return or incarnate upon the lower plane of Earth, they come back with inner knowledge and a subconscious that can guide them in their new life. Have you not wondered sometimes how you 'know' something that you also know you have not physically encountered it? Nothing dear friends, is wasted. All is put to good use somewhere!

We will leave that part of our discourse and transfer to the part where we left off, namely: 'you as a permanent being, existing in the world of the Spirit'.

You have been told by others, and read in books, that as Spirit you are 'beings of light', but what does that actually mean? The word 'light' has many connotations, it can be a 'beam', a 'vapour', an 'appearance'. In fact it can be all of those things and many, many more. Light here is an actuality by which we mean you, shall we say, manufacture it as you progress! It is part of you and yet can be separated from you and even given to someone who perhaps needs it for various reasons. Your light is not just an iridescent aura it is a 'tool' that can be used as you wish!

But how to use it has to be taught and learned before you can 'take charge' as it were, of this wonderful tool of light thought manipulation. As you know this realm is one of *thought,* everything stems from it, as it did when you dwelt upon Earth. You vibrate in thought, you transmit in thought and you live by thought! In other words, your thought patterns are seen as light emanations. So that a thought is reflected outwardly, each thought wave picks up its own vibrant colour and so you are continually changing, as it were.

We will now be more explicit. You wear 'garments', whatever is applicable to where you are, but these are no ordinary garments for they are made up of living light forces, do you begin to see where we are taking you? A garment of light force is a transmitter of your thought form. It reacts all the time. So you may, shall we say, start off with a garment of colour green, and as you progress through the passage of time, your thoughts automatically change that colour, which in turn gives off a living vibrant hue that others can see if they have progressed that far! Others may just be aware of a light vapour that seems to surround you as it does with all spirit forms whether they are aware of it or not.

So you see how important thought is. For here you are shown how to create what you would say is a physical object, which of course it is not. And yet it remains permanent for as long as it is needed. If not required any longer the thought object will just disappear, all part of this world of 'reality and illusions'. You have to remember that, and learn how to accept what is real and what is not exactly. Do not reject the illusion, for within it there may be a lesson for you to learn!

As you can see, life that you now live is unexpected, full of mystery and yet is as transparent as the wind! We return to your 'garment' which really is *you made visible,* as you progress so do the 'garments' that you acquire, and if you so wish, adornments that go with them. Remember though that none of this represents wealth, it just shows the position you have attained and nothing more. As you travel around our globe you will come across many beings of 'light', the colours of which will astound you, they are so beautiful and actually refresh you in your mind so that you feel better for having encountered them.

You will find that even buildings will have this effect upon you. They 'give off' what thoughts have created them and the thoughts of those who dwell within!

Everything in this world is made and created by living thought, that is why you will be affected by them. For in truth you are now part of not only where you are but of the very fabric of life itself!

There is so much more that we would like to tell you about but we have been informed that you have been given sufficient for the time being and so we will say to you our usual farewell.

Chapter 53

April 16th 2003

When to Teach!

Y ou were told in your previous discourse about the Spirit thought transference, an emanation that not only affects you but others also. *Thought* becomes a living form itself. Difficult for you to quite understand that, but it is a fact and a true one!

Thought here does not remain static in the mind. Once thought it becomes active, and here we talk 'constructive thought' not the, shall we say, mundane thoughts of the day! There are degrees of *thought*, for example those that are just for pleasure and *thought talk* in general!

Then there are the positive constructive thoughts that are to be used for a specific purpose, for example, for objects and for all creative activities also for the transference from one place to another! You do not always wish to use a mode of transport which is always available. In the quietude of your inward being, you may wish to travel, as it were, to somewhere beyond your immediate surrounding, even, shall we say, to another part of our globe of light. This is done in the form of a living thinking hologram type of identity! In other words, a non-permanent extension of your own Spirit body! This can be achieved by sustained thought and all impressions gained in this experience are conveyed back to the one who is doing the thinking! So you are, as it were, in two places at once. When you become proficient in this exercise you will be able to not only project this thought form but you yourself will remain actively participating in your every day life, so that those around you will have no idea of what is transpiring! All of these procedures have to be learnt if you wish to take advantage of this form of inward/outward travel!

It may be that you wish to avail yourself of either a particular form of knowledge or just to visit a particular place of interest that you have heard about. Now this 'hologram you' appears perfectly normal to those who you meet in these new surroundings and to all intents and purposes you *are you*! You behave as you normally would and when it is time for your thought form to return to its creator you will fade and disappear. But those who you have left have now understood the impression that you leave behind. For instance you may have found a new friend and if you wish to pursue this friendship then the 'creator you' can 'physically' materialise for as long as you wish where you wish! And your 'hologram you' can be if you wish returned to your permanent bode of habitation and so you are kept as it were in touch with your everyday activities!

So much for you to learn and appreciate. Though we must admit that not all Spirit entities wish to learn these things, at least not at first perhaps, but when they see the advantage of being and living in two places at the same time, they will no doubt take up this form of thought travelling. This all may seem strange to you as you read this, but to us it is quite 'normal' and believe us it is *true*!

Once in the world of the spirit there is so much freedom in every way, thought activities can be so rewarding. You learn from these experiences with others in the globe of light. All part of your character building, for believe us you still have your own character and it is forever being extended, for you have many journeys to take before you step forth into the next dimension on your upward path of understanding.

You are privileged, little friends upon the Earth, to be told of these things, some may gasp and say 'rubbish', that is because they do not wish to rethink their old thought patterns. But those of you who are the true seekers and searchers of inner knowledge will understand and accept what it is that we are allowed to impart to you. So if you talk with people about things of the Spirit, be wise and only give out what you feel they are able to accept. Never, never force your ideas and thoughts upon another human being, let them be the first to ask, for it will show you that they are on the path, and the thirst for inner knowledge can be assuaged by your thoughtful approach to any given subject! You are the *teachers* of this world, even if you are not aware of it, so remember always to impart what you know and feel is the *truth* for what you say may change another person's whole lifestyle. You have a duty not only to them, but to yourself also.

Truth! Always endeavour to speak that, but never to coerce another into your way of thinking. If they are ready, then you will know and if not, leave things as they are. For in time, God willing, they will seek out the one who can give them some answers to questions that have puzzled them for a long time!

Ask, before you give out your inner knowledge that what you say has the blessing of the One on High, for it is *His* work that you have chosen to do!

And here we will bid you farewell. Think upon these things and only accept what your inner self tells you is truth and correct.

Farewell little brothers upon the Earth and may you be blessed in the work that you do! Always be *yourselves*. Example is the best teacher in all things.

Chapter 54

April 18th 2003

You are You!

We will talk about 'freedom'. That is the freedom of the Spirit.

While you tarry upon the plane of Earth, your Spirit is somewhat like a prisoner in its own shell! It cannot roam at will as it is intended it should, for its prime object is the welfare of the human vehicle it has chosen while incarnating upon Earth.

You think you have freedom. Well up to a point you have. But it is nothing compared to the freedom that Spirit is heir to. Why then is not Spirit allowed this freedom that we speak of? 'It' has to learn about the restrictive practices of the mortal body. All for the purpose of learning, for that is why Spirit came to Earth, to learn and be taught and it achieves this by taking on this restrictive garment called body and once it does that, then its freedom is curtailed somewhat! Not completely but nevertheless it is restricted. And it does willingly, for it is aware that to limit itself is a lesson that needs to be learnt. It is a form of discipline. To show to Spirit that it has responsibilities far beyond its self. So the mortal body is chosen for this very purpose.

The planet called Earth is one of the many training grounds that Spirit must travel upon on its journey back to the essence we call soul. Even soul has not understood all about itself while upon the soul plane. It too needs this lesson of discipline! So it released the organ known to you as Spirit to accomplish this feat. It may take make incarnations on all the various spheres of existence before it attains this knowledge, but once achieved it is put to good use, for the soul can then resume its travel that has been interrupted by its sojourn upon the lower spheres. All part of the process we call learning. Soul as Soul is unrestricted, yet it is not aware of why it is so. It is the prime essence that God the Creator breathed into existence, a being without knowledge other than the fact that it is part of something much, much bigger and yet just what? It is unaware of its true identity, so that is the reason it has to come down to what may be termed reality! Reality of a gross body that can house it upon this lower plane called Earth.

Yet the soul itself remains on the soul plane as an identity in its own right, absorbing what is 'sent back to it' via its various incarnated bodies that it uses in the spheres below the soul plane.

Here we pause to say that there are more 'planes' above the soul plane, and once it has assimilated all of the knowledge that its other selves have acquired for it, it can now proceed to the higher realms with the knowledge of who it is and why it was created in the first place.

But dear friends, that form of existence is so far off that even to hint at it is forbidden! For in those realms you are in the domain of the most high, no longer a wandering species, you are where you belong and from where you originated!

Soul has willingly, though perhaps not knowingly, allowed itself to be isolated from the Father of all creation for the purpose of once again becoming part of Him who you call your God!

Each sphere that soul in spirit form inhabits restricts it more as it approached the Earth plane. The world that you know as Spirit is the last one before the Earth, and that one, the *Spirit*, is where *your* Spirit form dwells in part! You are, as it were, split in two and yet you are one in essence! Your Spirit has a certain amount of freedom while its body is incarnating upon Earth. But it is restricted somewhat, and yet it is learning and passing on this knowledge to its partner below who, in turn, though usually not aware, gives forth to Spirit what knowledge it is gaining and so both are progressing in unison. Spirit itself longs to be free of this earthly encumbrance but it understands the reasons for it and so accepts those limitations. Once released from the bondage of the earthly body, that is when it has eventually exhausted its rounds of life upon that plane, then its freedom is restored to it a hundred fold and more. It can now live in complete freedom of thought, though even that does have its limitations, but nothing like the Earth variety.

You still need to learn and be taught what these future lives hold for you. Some pass through this sphere quite rapidly while others tend to remain almost indefinitely. That is until they know that they must 'move on' if they intend to evolve as has been planned for them.

Though there are laws and suchlike upon the sphere of the spirit, you do have great freedom, not only of choice but of where you wish to be. You know that once here you gravitate, as it were, to those entities of a like mind. You may call them groups, or even part of a locality that houses them! You do not always remain with those that may have been your companions upon Earth.

Do not be despondent about that statement for your whole thought pattern is different from the one you used while in the lower body. You learn to accept what is! For you can see the logic of it all. Families can be reunited, even if it is only for, shall we say, reunions of old ties! Thoughts that bind but do not restrict or hold one back, so to speak. Your journey upon Earth has been one that should show you who you think you are, the Spirit one shows you who you *really are* or shall we say, have *become* and all because of this sojourn upon the lower plane. What seemed like restriction can now be seen in its true light, which was to instil in you a form of personal discipline that you yourself have acquired willingly.

Your spirit rejoices in all of this knowledge that is now put into practice, for without discipline of the self, your lessons have been in vain! Yet discipline need not be harsh if applied correctly. It is learning how to live and treat others in the right manner, putting aside selfish desires for the good of others.

Growing up, that is what you are doing. No longer a wayward child demanding without thought, but a thinking caring adult. One of Gods co-workers if you wish, for to do His work, however humble it may seem, shows that you do understand why you were created in the first place. So when you regain the freedom of the world of spirit, use it wisely and put into practice the lessons that you have learnt.

You are *you* and no one else! Accept your responsibilities and go forward in your new round of fulfilling lives!

Chapter 55

April 19th 2003

Angels!

A ngels! Can you tell me about them please? Are they real people or just wishful thoughts that a lot of people have?

Well dear friend, that is a tall order! For there are many degrees, as it were, in the angel hierarchy! There are those at the top, so to speak, who have never touched the Earth plane. They remain on a particular sphere where they perform duties for the Higher beings of light. They do move from planet to planet when required, for amongst their so-called duties is that of 'teacher'. They impart knowledge to those who are advanced in understanding. In other words they are helping those souls who are nearing the end of the souls journeying upon the various spheres! Not yours I'm afraid! Other spheres or planets are more advanced than yours and require a different form of tutors, if you like to put it that way.

They actually form a band of the Highest thought forms. They have always been and always will be *pure light forms* with extraordinary powers that would astound you as they do us! We do not *see* them but we can feel their influences. Then there are, shall we say, lesser angelic beings but 'lesser' does not mean what you may think, it just means that they are on a slightly lower vibration that the ones we talked of first.

These angels of light deal mainly with the lower worlds of human existence. Their job, as it were, is keeping order, or at least trying to. For all their powers, though great, they do not perform miracles. They observe the universe and work within it. It is their function to summon up forces of good that can be channelled down through other beings to the lower spheres of existence. They are, shall we say, 'working angels', for that is what they have been chosen for. These angels have been upon the Earth plane since many, many millennia ago and have progressed to this higher sphere through the sheer ability of their empathy with the lower forms of humanity.

There are various grades in this hierarchy. Some are beginners, others are what you would term 'old hands', all of them are teachers one way or another. They, in turn, live upon a sphere of light and their emanations are carried down to those who are waiting for the opportunity to be of service to mankind. We are only dealing with those upon the earth plane, the ones you call the humanities. Other planets have a different system to yours and so are of no practical interest to you at present.

Now we come to the angelic forces that your picture books show you. The ones in stained glass windows, these beings of light are the nearest ones to mankind, and perform many, many varied duties for mans benefit. Amongst them are those who you call 'guardian angels'. Though that word does not really convey what it is that they are allowed to do! They can watch over you and even influence your thoughts, but they are not allowed to make decisions for you. You have your own free will and the laws of the unseen universe have to be observed. Theirs, we feel, is the hardest job of all, for they cannot interfere with events that may transpire, or perhaps have been ordained as it were, by past events that result in perhaps some form of catastrophe or accident. They are allowed to try and help you avert what may seem to be an accident, or whatever has befallen a person!

You may get what you think of is an intuition that something untoward may happen, and so you perhaps do not go down that particular pathway, and so you avert a tragedy. Usually there is more than one choice that can be made and then the whole life cycle can be altered but not tampered with.

Do you understand what we say? Your guardian angel is, shall we say, an extension of yourself. One who has the ability to foresee events but cannot change them, only try to influence the thought patterns of the individual who they have always felt needed help and attention. That is why sometimes people will say 'well where was their guardian angel when that happened?' 'Makes you wonder if there are any if they can't help you when needed'.

This really is a hurtful thought for those angelic beings are doing all they can or are allowed to, and the people who criticise do not know the facts of any particular set of circumstances. So judge not that ye be not judged & found wanting!

There are other angelic beings in this category that are the inspiration for religious paintings, the ones you see pictured with wings. No they do not have them sprouting out from between their shoulder blades. But, they have the ability to create an illusion when it is deemed necessary and so that is the reason so many people prefer to think of angels as these celestial winged creatures. We see what we want to see and though we may *see* it, that does not mean that it is a reality!

We are sorry to perhaps disillusion those of you who prefer your angelic beings to be some form of winged apparition. Think of it practically and you will soon realise the impracticability of the whole idea, however appealing to the senses it may be! And we do admit that when you see pictures of angels with wings folded or outstretched they are aesthetically very appealing. But that is all!

Have we exhausted our talk of angels? Well no! For there are many more that can be termed 'angels' but they need not be of the Spirit variety. Angels can be just ordinary people upon your Earth. It is what a person *is* that makes them what you term angel.

So think upon that. Who knows, your neighbour may be one, or the bent and laboured person who you pass in the street! They don't need a label for God to see their worth, being who they *are* is enough for Him to recognise the one who could qualify for the word 'an angel'!

We feel that we have given you another insight into what other realms have amongst their inhabitants, just the same as you have upon your Earth!

Chapter 56

April 25th 2003

Time

Turn back the pages of your mind to when you were a young man.

Do you remember asking for the truth? The answer that you received was 'the truth shall make you free'. Yes, you do remember and so do we!

That no doubt surprises you, for in those days you had no knowable knowledge of the deeper esoteric understanding of what life was all about. You had yearnings but you did not know how to go about pursuing what it was that seemed to elude you. You were, dear brother, on the threshold, as it were, of discovering not only yourself but the meaning of why you are here upon the Earth plane in the first place!

Yet at that time you were not quite ready, time had to pass before you were in a position to understand the deeper meanings. Such things do not come about, as it were, in a flash of inspiration. Learning is gradual. It has to be if it is to be of lasting value! Time to us is of no real importance as it is to you upon the Earth. It does have its place like all things, but time is a flexible piece of machinery and can be slowed, made fast or obliterated altogether if the occasion arises!

Difficult perhaps for you to quite understand as you upon the Earth are governed, as it were, by 'time'. To us it is merely a 'passage' from one situation to another and time in that sense can be manipulated as we wish, *but* we cannot alter your *time scale*!

We can ignore it if we wish, and shall we try to explain to you how this is done? It is a form of 'sleep'! Not quite as you know it, but we can as it were form a barrier between ourselves and the one who we are in the process of 'teaching'. Which dear friend, and Brother is *you* of whom we speak! Your span of time between those days of your youth and the ones to which you now occupy, which have been your true awakening, were to us but a day's passing! No, not quite literally but you understand our meaning, do you not?

Your passage of time in the form of years spent upon Earth were times of 'growing up', not only physically but Spiritually as well. It all takes time, when upon the Earth, for what is being taught and learnt by the 'Spirit' cannot be thrust upon the inner thought process without due consideration as to how it would be accepted!

Do you follow? Too much too soon would be overwhelming for your intellectual abilities. You have to come to certain conclusions in a gradual fashion. What is perhaps learnt at one period, may lay dormant until re-awakened at a later time when, you are more receptive, and what was learnt is now relevant to where you are now!! You may think to yourself, what were we doing during this period between youth and maturity of your body?

We said it was a form of 'sleep' as far as we are concerned, but that did not mean that we were inactive on your behalf. We have many 'pupils' if you like to think of yourself as one! All progressing at different stages, and so we go as it were from 'one to another' during what we have termed the 'sleep process' in other words we 'come and go' as we feel we are needed by our protégés! We monitor each one over the 'years' that is *your years* not ours.

We see how your life is affecting you. How you are learning and adapting to various circumstances and how they are affecting your mental/spiritual attitudes. We have, as it were, a 'liaison' between ourselves and your physical body which is not only your own spirit counterpart but also your 'guide and helper', whoever they are and whatever name you wish to call them! Some might say 'guardian angel'. Just depends on your viewpoint! Nevertheless 'they' or 'he' is the one who is observing and guiding you, and 'he' it is that informs us of your progress whenever we wish to be brought up to date with what is befalling you. You are *never* alone, even when you feel you are! Spiritually you are always being nurtured and taken care of, even if at the time you may feel shall we say 'forsaken'!

So you see dear friend we are fully aware of your progress and when we are told the 'time is right', then we, as it were, manifest ourselves to you Spiritually for you are now in the awakened stage and ready to receive the higher knowledge and understanding!

We awaken within you the desire for more knowledge. Knowledge that you already have but are not yet aware of! You have learnt and earned this knowledge through the course of your years upon Earth. You are now in a position to be 'used' as an instrument of teaching to others what is not only given to you from your brothers in Christ but also from your own inner self. Knowledge that is from the 'Christ Consciousness' is always the *truth* whether from outside or inside the one who is being used to impart it! Which, little Brother, is *you*. It is now your turn to instruct! Do not doubt either yourself or us. For we are all on the one path, back to our Creator. You are *not alone* in this enterprise, and you do know that, don't you?!

Your life was mapped out by not only us but with your co-operation long, long before you two were jointed together to embark upon the work chosen for you by the One on High!

One day soon, you will be able to see the results of your lifetime's study and work and, yes little friend, you will be able to feel proud of the achievement of both of you!

Proud, but not Pride. We know you understand the meaning of that statement!

Yes dear friend 'things' are to be 'speeded up', so just accept what may be happening to you and around you. You are being guided and protected. Have no fear, put your trust not only in the *Lord your God* but also in Us his servants, and your brothers!

Peace be with you.

Chapter 57

April 27th 2003

Talk to God

It would seem that as we approach the end of life's journey upon Earth, we think back to the days when we were young. When life was full of promise and we didn't even wonder what lay in store for us. Perhaps that is a good thing, for if we did know what the life ahead had waiting for us we might have given up there and then! So in Gods mercy we do not know, at least the physical part of us is kept in ignorance, and what a mercy that is if we did but know it!

It is only after perhaps many ups and downs that come our way that we learn how to combat them and yes, overcome them. It is only when we look back upon those earlier days that we begin to see a pattern and we realise that we needed all those so called 'ups and downs' for they have made us what we are today as we review what our life has meant to us.

Do you perhaps wonder and think 'was it all worth it?' Have I really learnt what it is that I came to Earth for? And am I now fit to proceed upon the next stage of my journey through the lives that await me?!

More often than not, many people won't even think along those lines. Their whole life has been spent living it, or trying as best they can to, and so they have had no time in which to try and evaluate what life has taught them, or should have taught them is more to the point!

They do not wish to know why it is that they come here to live and learn. All they know is that they have, and as far as they are concerned that is all there is to it! When the end is in sight, they may think vaguely what the next stage will be like, but it is only vague thoughts that assail their minds. 'Heaven' is what most people believe is the next step and that word means so many different things to so many people!

Usually it is thought of as some form of reward for having lived through the life upon Earth, as if that life was some form of purgatory and the one to come will erase all the hurtful memories of it!

Well, that may be what to most people is what will happen to them. And if you were to probe deeper into their inner thoughts about the next chapter in their life's journey, they would not be able to give you a really concrete idea of what they think awaits them, let alone what life has taught them, and fitted them for this next stage in the upward search for answers to what life, or rather *lives*, are all about.

They don't really want to think too deeply about it, for if they did, they might not like what it is that they see! This Earth life has been one of preparation for the one to come, and so what has transpired to an individual must have relevance to it, mustn't it?

It has been left to the searchers and seekers and, yes, the thinkers of this world to try and make sense of it all. And believe us dear friends, to some, this life of theirs seems to have made very little sense when they think of where it is leading them to! Such a pity, for we have been endowed with intelligence and a brain to bring that intelligence into some form of cohesive thinking. The life to come really has been one that takes in all that has befallen a person while upon the Earth. It has made them what they are and so we should all be aware of why we are here, and why living upon the Earth is so important to our development, for it is who and what we are that is to fit us for the next part of our life's journey! If we have truly understood what our life has been for, then we may be in a position to not need to return to this lower sphere of learning, for our lessons would have been learnt. Sadly though, many souls have not learnt all they should have and so their stay in what you like to term 'Heaven' would only be a passing one and not one of permanence.

If people of the West were to understand the true meaning of 'life' and why we have chosen to live it upon this planet called Earth, they would perhaps see their lives here in a very different state. People in the Eastern regions have certain ideas about what awaits them when death overtakes this mortal body. But even their ideas are flawed, so very few people really understand what this and the future lives are really all about! Yet, can they be blamed for their thinking?

We say, no, they cannot, for the teachings of those of the various religious orders do very little to enlighten them as to the true reality for their existence whether here or elsewhere! Everything is clouded in a form of either mystery or at best second hand knowledge, which in most cases cannot be verified to an individuals satisfaction.

Religious teaching in every known case, needs to be 'overhauled' as it were. What was relevant thousands of years ago, is not relevant to today. What was a truth then cannot stand up to today's scrutiny!

That is not to say that it was not the truth, for it was then, but it is seen in a completely different light in today's modern outlook on life and what it means. The young of today and yes, those who are yet to be born, are seeking answers. Answers that will satisfy their curiosity and the feelings that they have that life is more than just this life that they are living. It has to make sense to them and at present it does not! And all because of the thinking of the past!

Past is past! It has its place in the world's history but it must not be dwelt upon as if it is the only way of looking at life and its teachings. You have to move on if you want to progress, and that means your thinking, and what it does for you! For when you start to think and we mean really *start to think* then you will begin to live life as it was intended to be lived!

And yes, as it can be lived, but that does mean a change in the way that you look at what life is all about!

Make life worth living, and that does mean for *all peoples* and not just for the fortunate few. We hesitate to bring the word *God* into this conversation, for too many people that is just a word and the true meaning of it is lost, but that is just what is lacking in today's thinking. You no longer look to *God* for guidance, yet He is very much *alive* contrary to what many so called academics would have you think. They put forth theories regarding life, birth, death and all the trappings that go with it and either dismiss the idea of a divine Creative force or put forward ideas that may seem plausible, but in reality have no substance whatsoever!

People *must* learn to think for themselves, for truly within them lies the true answer to most of their questions, and the answer would mean re-thinking what perhaps has always been thought of as sacrosanct. *Thoughts* are for thinking about and doing something about, not just idle speculation and then left on the shelf so to speak.

You are here for a purpose and that purpose is *God's* and not your own! Learn to accept that you are a part of *God's* plan and there's no getting away from it. You are a part of *God* as *He* is a part of you. Begin to accept that fact and you will find that not only do things fall into place but they also make sense.

Once God was talked about freely, even if He was thought of as somewhat vengeful if you didn't obey Him. Thank goodness those thoughts no longer persist, but He still does; and He does, with *Love*, always with *Love*.

God and love are synonymous with life and reality for one

without the other is not complete. We all need *love* and we all *need* *God*. Even if you think you are beyond that concept, you are not. You only delude yourself.

Bring *God* back into your lives. Don't be ashamed to talk about him, for if you did but know it most people *want* to believe, but do not know how and will not allow themselves to speak to *God*. It doesn't have to be with the spoken word, a thought is all that is needed to get in touch with the Divinity. Bring *Him* into your every day thinking and you will be surprised at how what may have seemed a burden in life can be either lifted or at best viewed for what it is. Do not despair and when you 'fall' ask *God* for help and you will get it, even if it is not quite how you expect it to come about!

We feel that that is where we will leave you for this nights discourse.

Chapter 58

May 1st 2003

Think Ahead

L ife to so many people is somewhat perplexing. They have enough to do day in and day out just keeping, in your expression, 'the wolf from the door' and so they have not the inclination to stop and think 'where am I going'? 'Where is all this effort leading me to?' And the last thought in their minds is what will come after their life upon Earth when the end is in sight! And when it is, to most people it is too late to really understand what the so-called spirit world is all about! They either close their minds on the subject or feel what's the use of their worrying, its going to happen anyway.

Not very philosophical we feel! For you are going to embark upon a new life. A new round of experiences. So why not try and find out what this new life will involve? Of course this should all have been thought about long before the so-called end of life is beckoning! And really it is not the end but a new beginning, if they could only realise it.

Death is merely the gateway that we all have to pass through. It is the manner in which we have to pass is what makes most people apprehensive about their passing. We grant you, as you do not know of how that event is to come about it is natural for one to be not only worried but also somewhat apprehensive as to the outcome. It is a merciful thing that we do not know exactly how that event will take place.

Some people are forewarned when perhaps they have a terminal illness and are given just so long in which to adjust to the inevitable. They are, shall we say, the fortunate ones, for they can prepare themselves and in these days you have what you call 'hospices' which we consider wonderful places for the adjustment of not only the body but the mind and the spirit also!

We think of them as not only 'rest homes' but as 'waiting rooms' before proceeding to the next phase in life's journey. These places of rest make our 'job' so much easier when the body has been left behind and the Spirit is free to resume its interrupted journey. This pre-period of adjustment is so necessary in fact if all people could have some form of this time of re-evaluating their life's work then the transition from one sphere to the next would be so much easier. Perhaps one day there will come a time when ordinary folk will be able to 'take time off', as it were, when they are nearing their transition stage and go into the solitude of a quiet rest place so that they can adjust themselves and also those who will be left behind. Mourning, though acceptable need not be one of sadness, for the release of the mortal body to a finer one should be viewed with joy, and after all it is only as if the loved one is going on ahead to prepare a place for those left behind.

One day, it has been promised, all people will dwell in both worlds simultaneously and so this feeling of 'loss' will no longer be the same as is experienced now. For though the 'loved one' has, shall we say, 'moved on', they will still be visible to those left behind. Not shall we say on a permanent basis for they will have their new life to get on with, but there will be 'times' when thoughts unite and then loved ones can come together for a brief span.

But all of this is in the far off future, when mankind has become more Spiritually orientated! In actual fact, in those days of the past when man was less materialistic and you would call him perhaps 'primitive', he was more in touch with those in the world of spirit. But he has lost that ability of unification that he had, and he has to search for what he thinks of as the unknown, where, if he did but realise it, it is still within his grasp. But he must re-think what he has grown to accept as a facet of the truth, which after all is only one facet, and there are many that go to make a complete 'truth'!

When man learns to accept that he is not only a physical body but also a Spiritual one and that one should be the guiding force in his living, plan for the future life by learning about it. You don't have to hurry towards it, but you can learn more about it and in doing so your physical life will improve beyond your wildest dreams. For you will then understand why you are living upon this Earth, which is the one of preparations for the permanent one to come.

You may regret leaving this Earth life when it is your time to vacate it but think of the glorious one to come and know that that life will be the true one and that you will then begin to really *live*. Death of the physical body is natural and inevitable and not to be looked upon with horror. To die is to live again, and this time with a body of light and no restrictions of any sort.

Live as best you can while upon the Earth, for it is the training ground for your next one on the higher realm of Spirit.

We leave you on that note, dear friends, and we leave you with our blessings from the One on High.

Chapter 59

May 4th 2003

Unknown Area's

Welcome Brother, welcome.

The other night in the discourse, we said at the end that we would in due course inform you of the so-called 'unknown areas' that still exist upon our world of the Spirit. You were surprised that there were any 'unknown' areas, for you imagined that the Spirit world must be, shall we say, open with no hidden areas. Most people would feel the same way, but dear friend, look around your own world. There are still some areas that have not been fully explored and remain, as it were, hidden from view.

In spite of your advancement in transport you have not yet penetrated those dark and mysterious forests that still cling to your Earth. We wonder though for how long! For you seem bent on destroying what, in reality, is part of 'life's blood'. Once those forests have gone that is it! You cannot replace in a decade what has taken hundreds of years to produce.

Well that is all up to you. You think you know what you are doing but you only look at the short term, not the long term which is the one that you should be concerned about.

Now to return to our world, which I can assure you is better managed than your own! We see everything as part of 'us', all given from the One on High. We care for what has been given to us and so we profit from what we are allowed to use and yes, 'partake' of. For we know that all of the life force that we enjoy is not only all around us but within us too.

We spoke of the 'unknown areas' that still exist upon our planet. That should not surprise you really, for 'our world' is far larger than yours and has far more diversity than you could ever imagine. Our plant life would amaze you, for its properties that not only nourish but also 'heal'. You think, why should we need 'healing properties' surely Spirit people do not need healing? You, dear friend, are thinking only of the 'body' which we do assume when needed. No, it is the 'mind' of which we talk! The mind is carried over from the lower sphere, your Earth plane, and does not automatically become all knowing, for you have spent a lifetime upon Earth using it for purposes of 'living' and so it has, shall we say been imprisoned in the thought process and not allowed the freedom to express itself and explore its potentials! When we encounter such souls who need that form of re-adjusting and also 'counselling', then we have the means to help and heal them and start them in their new lifestyle!

So you see, our plant forms are very special to us. We cultivate them, and incidentally there maybe what you term a 'spin off', where we feel that you upon the Earth plane could benefit from our work. There are plants and life forms that are grown here that could be adapted to your Earth's atmosphere, and so you will in due time 'come across' these species, some of which are already growing in the depths of your forests. These are all for medicinal purposes and will replace some of your own synthetic drugs that seem to have 'side effects' while ours have only beneficial properties and have no such things as 'side effects'.

This is just one of our growth forms. We send out to some of these 'unknown areas' people who specialise in the knowledge of different species and organisms that they find, and incidentally, they do encounter the inhabitants of these areas, who are most helpful to us. No, they are not primitive people, they live and work with what you upon Earth call 'Nature'. They teach us and we in turn teach them. We do not intrude upon their lifestyle. We exchange ideas and if any of them wish to accompany us when we return to our part of the globe, they are free to do so. It has been known that some of our parties chose to remain with our brothers of the forest, so you see it is a two way exchange not only of ideas but of persons also.

There are other areas that astound us with their knowledge and achievements. We are continually learning about new techniques, not only of our world but of other worlds also. Though we are what you like to call Spirit, we are still 'human' if that is the right word, which it is not but that will do for now.

In one of those 'areas' we have seen how people can be 'transported' and yet 'remain' where they are. They understand the principles of assembling the molecules of the 'body' and then re-aligning them elsewhere while still retaining the original. All to do with the substance of the 'mind' and the owner of that substance, if you follow what we are saying.

These areas are purely for scientific purposes and are not known about by, shall we say, 'ordinary people'. They are for those with academic ability from all over our planet. They are 'teaching schools' where whole families live and, if wanted to, learn. Their dwelling places are not exactly 'Spartan', but they only create what they feel they need. Most are single storey buildings with a central courtyard or sometimes a form of 'lawn' where most of the everyday activity takes place. There are areas put aside for what you would term 'rest' which has no set period or for that matter 'time'. Nourishment is all around them in the 'air' that they breathe, but 'food' as you perhaps call it can be produced and eaten if and when they desire it. Children seem to like the change, and the adults allow them to enjoy something that is different for them and yes, they also enjoy the change! Food though, as we have told you before, is not of the 'solid variety'. It may appear so and the 'sensation' is there but that is all. The body as such does *not* require your sort of substance, as we do not also!

There are still areas, in fact whole continents, that are still to be explored, and we do not know what and who we will find in our exploration. We only know that we will benefit from this venture, as will those who we may encounter.

So you see dear Brother, life here is full of adventure and excitement and through it all 'learning'. Learning who we are and about our relationship with each other. Life goes on, it does *not* stand still. It never has and it never will, wherever we may find ourselves in our evolutionary progress.

Chapter 60

June 29th 2003

Life or Lives?

We will begin this discourse by saying life is a training ground.

Perhaps we should have said *lives*, not just life! For we have many, many lives on our way back to where we started out from on our journey of discovering the purpose of our very existence. And you have thought, *why*? What is it all for, this melange of our various lives! And you think, just what are they telling you if you cannot remember them in sequence!

Well dear friend, you do. At the right time. And that is when one incarnation has been completed and you are back in the realm of Spirit for rest and rejuvenation of the Spirit. For believe us, your Spirit has had to undergo quite a lot while it was tarrying in your physical body! Many people think that it is this physical body that has to incarnate upon Earth to gain experience and knowledge, but that is only the half of it! For the Spirit also has to be further educated, for that is the real 'substance' that goes from realm to realm in its pursuit of perfection and understanding.

Your body is just a vehicle of use for the Spirit to gain knowledge of the lower plane of existence! And in the learning, it becomes just that little bit wiser about itself. In fact it is learning *how* to live a fuller life that will equip it for an even fuller one on one of the many planes that it will encounter in its journey back to its source of all Creation!

You wonder just what part *you*, as an individual, play in this role you call 'life' and do you really matter?

The answer is a resounding *YES YOU DO MATTER*!

You will not be able to understand just how that will come about but believe us, dear friend, it is the Truth. *We all matter* to the One on High! We cannot explain 'how' for we do not know that answer. If we did then we would not be in this position of teaching others, for we would be what we all strive to be part of the ultimate. In fact we would *be* the ultimate!

But that explanation can never be explained while we are still in the body, either *physical* or *Spiritual*, or in one of the many other so called *bodies of light*. All words to try and explain what in reality is unexplainable to mortal man! Or His Spirit counterpart for that matter!

So much you see, dear Brother, has to be taken on *Trust*. Not what you are *told* but what *you* feel for yourself *inside*. In other words your *Spirit you*. You are in possession of far more knowledge and understanding than you realise, and here we are referring not just to you, our dear Brother, but to all of the thinking brethren all over your Earth globe and yes, even *beyond it*! We tend to forget that we are not the only forms of the humanities that have been created for Gods unknowable purpose.

As creatures who dwell upon the Earth and its satellite that is called the Spirit World, we tend to think only in terms that affect *us*. But beyond our little universe, and here we speak not about *the universe* but just our own little domain, and yet there are many such *little domains* that go to make up the completed one! That is known as our universe. But have you not thought that perhaps there are many more than just the one that we are part of?

To many people that concept would be unthinkable! But is it? Why should there be *only* one *universe*? The same as why should there be only one known world of human existence?

So much to think about, isn't there? And you begin to wonder what good will it do you to try and work out what almost seems an impossible task.

So that is where *trust* comes in! There is so much that we can never really know and explain to not only ourselves but also to others, so there comes a time when we must cry '*Halt*', and leave it at that. For we are *not* programmed in this life to fathom out all the hidden mysteries of what *life* is all about and what it is really for, and why it is in the first place!

Dear Brother, learn to accept your limitation. That is not to say that you must cease your thinking and wondering, but *know* that you will never in this life receive all of the answers that you crave for, and believe us that is for *your own good*. *We know* from personal experience so we do speak with authority on that subject.

Carry on thinking little Scribe, for that is what you were put upon your Earth to do. As you are now aware. We all have a reason for being where we are at a given time in our physical life, and yes, even in our Spiritual one as well! For in reality *all* of our lives have a meaning to them, and one day we will see them for what they are and where they have brought us to in our form of so called evolution. For that evolution is not just for the physical, it encompasses *all* of our 'bodies of light'. We have to say 'bodies' for that is how we tend to think of ourselves as, and how human beings can understand, for the term '*light*' does not really convey a meaningful explanation of who and what we are really *made of*!

And even the word 'light' doesn't really help you does it? You want to be able to identify what you term a *body* as a *body* not as a substance that is not only ethereal and Spiritual, but one that you can say 'yes, I know who and what I am! There again we have to say that word *Trust*. And know that we are *all* of a Spiritual substance, or essence, just as your God is.

Do not try to think any further, little Brother, just accept and know that you are *not* alone in your thinking and wondering. You have joined a band of like-minded beings and we are truly *all Brothers* in this union of Souls!

We feel that we will now depart from this night's discourse, for you have much to think about have you not?

Printed in the United Kingdom
by Lightning Source UK Ltd.
108810UKS00001B/109-126